CareerCode

KNOW YOUR CODE, FIND YOUR FIT

Jan Lowe and Tracy Lungrin

BEAVER'S POND
PRESS

ISBN: 978-1-59298-468-8
Library of Congress Control Number: 2012904878

Book design by Ryan Scheife, Mayfly Design
Printed in the United States of America
First Printing: 2012

16 15 14 13 12   5 4 3 2 1

BEAVER'S POND
PRESS

Beaver's Pond Press, Inc.
7108 Ohms Lane, Edina, MN 55439-2129
(952) 829-8818 • www.BeaversPondPress.com

To order, visit www.BeaversPondBooks.com or call (800) 901-3480.
Reseller discounts available.

"As a professional career coach and author, I make a point of re
career-related books all the time. But what made *CareerCode*
ent was that I didn't just read it, I reread it—twice. It quickly b
clear to me that this is a system that is simple without being si
tic, logical without being rigid, and ambitious without being ut
The result is a powerful set of tools for understanding what
you tick and what has been holding you back all these years. I
recommend this book to everyone wishing to take control of
working life in an intelligent, organized, and authentic way. "

—Jane Downes, author of *The Career*
Help for the Restless

"I am thrilled to have something this spot on and comprehens
support folks in their job search, job transition, and career dev
ment. Focusing on finding the right job based on your Career
will help career seekers to meet these challenges head on. This
mation is a must.... It is like a roadmap for your career life."

—Kathryn Johnson, executive rec

"Finding a great job is like finding a great hat: you know when it
because it makes you look and feel your best. But what if you
forty thousand hats to choose from—in the dark? The likelihoo
poor fit is daunting. Jan and Tracy have 'cracked the code' to fir
your optimal job fit. This is the most efficient way I've ever four
identify your next best job match. The only question I ask a pe
without their CareerCode is: Just how long do you want to tr
random hats in the dark?"

—Brad Lee Thompson, founder and CEO of Labels 2 Le
author of *Concise Handbook for New Managers* and other b

Contents

Introduction

We want you to know why the two of us—Tracy and Jan—felt so compelled to write this book.

In July 2000, we met in our home state of Nebraska. We had an instant personal connection and soon discovered that we shared a passion for vocational counseling.

Jan's career began in the early 1970s, when she worked as a vocational rehabilitation counselor for the state of Minnesota after earning her master's degree in vocational rehabilitation counseling. For more than thirty-five years, she has been an expert witness in cases involving employability—analyzing how individuals, with their education, experience, and interests, fit into the job market. During her career, she has prepared reports for thousands of court cases. Jan has worked primarily with people who are making a job change—specifically, displaced workers and midlife career changers. She has been called on to evaluate and testify about earning capacity based on vocational qualifications and about "career fit."

Tracy earned a master's degree in counseling and college student development. She began her career as a college admissions counselor and quickly noticed how much time students and families spend on the college admissions and financial aid processes, yet how little time they devote to career planning. She would often hear from former students who were floundering after college because they felt so unprepared for the "real world." She noticed how her own educational program lacked in preparing high school and college students for the world of work. Believe it or not, career counseling is not offered as an area of specialization in the vast majority of counselor training programs. As a result, Tracy watched hundreds of students and families make large financial investments with little awareness about employment and no plan of attack to find a career path.

Even though we are both trained as counselors, we have worked with different sets of clients. While their ages and life experiences seem light-years apart, they all share one critical trait: *career struggles.*

We've worked with thousands of people—young adults as well as workers nearing retirement who have encountered similar problems finding their sense of purpose, identifying the right career, and pursuing it with a plan. We know how scary the labor market can seem when you lack information, understanding, and confidence. We also realize that there has been no easily accessible approach available for the general public to explore and evaluate a person's fit in the world of work—*until now!*

CareerCode is a guide for…

- the student seeking career direction;
- the worker in an unsatisfying career path, seeking options for a better career fit;
- the retiree looking for a job or volunteer opportunity with a sense of purpose;
- the parent, spouse, or significant other who wants to support a student, career changer, or a retiree in finding a place in the labor market or the world of volunteer possibilities; and
- our peers in the helping professions of education and vocational counseling.

Millions of people have taken vocational interest tests in their quest for a satisfying career path; however, taking an interest test does not guarantee an understanding of the results or their use in making vocational decisions. *Career-Code* offers an easy-to-understand method of interpreting vocational interest test results, and it identifies and characterizes six Interest Codes to build individualized Code-Combos and CareerCodes, which can then be applied to people and jobs. These tools help provide the definition and assurance to end the career gridlock and begin each person's unique and individual journey.

Know your code and find your fit!

CHAPTER 1

An Identity Crisis

When Jade came into our office, she was at a crossroads in her life and her career. For years, she'd been working in an unsatisfying job. She was bogged down by the emotional pain of a divorce. Jade knew it was time to reinvent her life; but when it came to her career, she faced two unappealing paths: stay on course and experience more days of feeling unfulfilled, or branch off in a new direction into the job market—the confusing and overwhelming world full of risk and terrifying uncertainty.

How would she ever find contentment?

She'd gotten into her predicament by going against her better instincts, following the well-meaning but misguided advice of others, and choosing a college track and a career for reasons that weren't true to her own desires but seemed to make sense at the time: what paid well, what seemed to offer security, and more importantly, what others expected of her. Indeed, she had found a high-paying career with plenty of security. But she was miserable. She felt aimless, unmotivated. Her career lacked a meaningful connection with what she wanted to do with her life; she lacked a sense of purpose.

When Jade was growing up, her father had a successful career working for the state as an economist. He made a nice living and encouraged all his children to attend college. When it was time to enroll in school, Jade wanted to study fashion design. But her father did not approve; he had no idea how a designer could earn a living. He said he'd only pay for her education if she followed him into business or economics, two paths he knew would pay well.

So Jade put her desires aside and earned her economics degree. But when she graduated, she had little interest in going into the field. Instead, she gravitated back to her original dream, starting her own freelance design business. She soon realized she was in over her head. She was inexperienced, and she lacked training. When she couldn't support herself, she relented and took a job with the government.

The job was a perfect match for her degree, but not for Jade as a person. She earned good money, and yet she was unhappy. Over the years, she moved up through the ranks of the agency, but none of the promotions fed the true hunger inside her. People who get promotions and make good money are supposed to feel invigorated, right? That's what we are led to believe. Well, not Jade. She felt empty and drained. Many of the people close to her couldn't understand why.

Again, her passion for creative projects called to her. She quit her job and took a year off to pursue projects that fed her soul. Jade went to her stash in the closet and pulled out fabric, trims, buttons, and beads. She crafted pillows, scarves, and jewelry, spending hours lost in her designs. Unfortunately, she started running out of money, and her husband became tired of her "vacation." She looked for work but once more was forced onto a path that didn't suit her. The only employers who showed interest in her were those with jobs that matched her education and employment background—in economics.

Jade felt trapped and pushed by her family to pursue a career for which she had no passion. She knew her dad meant well when he urged her to study economics, but she resented him for shoving her in a direction she didn't want to go. Her career discontent even played a role in the demise of her marriage; she was so frustrated and discouraged about her work life that it bled into her personal life. "Much like my dad," she explained, "my ex-husband is a successful professional. He simply could not understand how I could be so unhappy when I was making such a good living." Not only was she discontented at work, but she was increasingly alienated from the people who were important to her.

Unfortunately, the frustration, uncertainty, and self-defeat Jade felt are not uncommon. In fact, many people can relate to her dilemma.

Just as it did for Jade, the pressure of choosing a career path begins at a young age for all of us, arguably at a time in our life when we are emotionally unprepared to handle such a significant and life-defining decision.

Work is an incredibly important part of life in nearly every culture. One reason career selection is so important is because, in a sense, we declare what our contribution to the world will be—whether as a doctor, teacher, or machine operator. What is one of the first things people ask each other when meeting for the first time? "What do you do for a living?"

We know from meeting with hundreds of people seeking career counseling that when people are not purposely aligned with what they do, they begin to lack pride in who they are. What someone does for a living is an expression of who he or she is as a person. We are not all alike, and we each have different gifts to use as we interact with family, friends, community, and the workplace. But we don't always know how to find our way.

Regardless of age, career unhappiness wreaks havoc on people's lives. Career indecision is like getting lost in an unknown environment. When we feel lost, we start to panic. We begin to doubt ourselves. We feel unsure and self-conscious about every move.

Our clients have told us that career uncertainty makes them feel vulnerable, lost, and alone. They begin to doubt themselves, saying, "Everyone else has a plan. Why don't I?" Career issues can cause major problems in interpersonal relationships, just as it did for Jade, whether it be with family, friends, significant others, or coworkers. The overwhelming feeling of helplessness and hopelessness rings true for so many of our clients.

The CareerCode Solution

CareerCode is a unique process that first allows people to understand themselves in relation to the world of work. In order to find a suitable career path, you need to understand yourself and the type of work environment that will be the best fit.

The vocational psychology behind CareerCode isn't new. In fact, it's as old as some baby boomers. It was developed in the 1950s by Dr. John Holland at Johns Hopkins University. What *is* brand new is the way we can show you how to apply it to your life.

The world of work and education looks almost nothing like the way it did fifty years ago. For one thing, the sheer variety of options has exploded—and they keep growing. There are more than forty thousand different jobs in the United States, each having a unique title and description as well as responsibilities and requirements. We're not talking about job *openings* here. We're talking about job titles and roles, such as veterinarian or computer programmer or legal assistant. There are many more job openings than there are job types.

New titles and roles are created every year. A few years ago you couldn't make money as a blogger-for-hire, or a cell phone video engineer, or a director of distribution for pay-per-view video downloads. We live in a constantly changing labor market.

Just as you need a map to find your way to an unfamiliar location, you need a map to find your way in the labor market. We have spent years studying Dr. Holland's timeless theory. In fact, we have been a bit obsessive in our quest. These codes have been like a Rubik's Cube for us during the past six years (just ask our families). We have done a great deal of research and written hundreds of emails. We have talked for hours on end about our experiences and interviews with hundreds of people, including our clients, students, family, and friends, until we finally put all the pieces together.

We were determined to dissect this theory in a way so you can have the same "aha" experience we felt. Our mission is simple: to offer you insight into *who* you are, to help define *what* you are seeking, and to help explain *why* other paths will not work.

We are very excited to share these revelations with you, so that you can now feel empowered to go after what will make you the happiest and most successful.

What Is CareerCode?

Each individual has a CareerCode comprised of letters from six different interest areas. The sequence and weighting of the code for each of these six areas is used to construct your individualized CareerCode. Your personal CareerCode empowers you in three different ways:

1. **Your one-letter Interest Code** identifies your general approach to life and work, as well as the things that most interest and motivate you. There are six Interest Codes:

    - **R (Realistic)**
    - **I (Investigative)**
    - **A (Artistic)**
    - **S (Social)**
    - **E (Enterprising)**
    - **C (Conventional)**

    Do you like to work with your hands and fix things? That's an R tendency. Are you driven to share information with others? You have some S in you. Finding out which of these codes applies to you is the first step in determining the educational programs and jobs that are best for you.

2. **Your two-letter CodeCombo** identifies which of thirty very different CodeCombos best describes you. Knowing your CodeCombo takes you deeper than your one-letter Interest Code and enables you to zero in on who you are and what you enjoy doing. It will lead to jobs and career paths where you are most likely to thrive. (Chapters 4 through 9 of this book describe these thirty interest profiles in more detail.)

3. **Your three-, four-, five-, and six-letter Career-Codes** further define your best fit in the labor market. They also clarify what you *don't* enjoy. This can be just as important as knowing what you love. Even though it is important to understand the concept of adding additional codes to the CodeCombo, the focus of this book will primarily be the two-letter CodeCombos.

Discovering your top Interest Code and your Career-Code is easy. The entire process is laid out in the pages that follow. It takes about ten to twenty minutes and requires nothing more than a little reading and thinking.

CHAPTER 2

What You're Up Against

We ended the previous chapter with good news. And there's much more good news to come—but first we need to deliver some bad news. You need to know what you're up against in the evolving labor market. The career planning process that nearly everyone still uses is completely backward. It's usually built around what other people think you are—or should be—rather than who you actually are.

From the time we're young, other people—our parents, relatives, friends, and teachers—tell us who and what we are. And some of our clients have experienced more pressure than others. In many interviews, people tell us they have heard the following:

"You're so smart; you're going to be a lawyer, just like your mom."

"We need you to take over the family business."

"Of course you'll go to Dartmouth—all your brothers and sisters did."

"Your mother and I will be so proud of you when you join the Air Force."

"You're incredibly talented. Are you saying you'd rather waste your talent than go to art school?"

From the time you're born, people have expectations for you, and they're rarely shy about making them known. Nobody understands this more than Sam, one of Jan's mid-career clients.

Sam's Story

Sam was raised in a rural Illinois community. His father was a production manager at the manufacturing plant, and his mother worked as an accountant. Sam was very studious and earned good grades during his undergraduate years. He majored in biology and psychology and completed his bachelor's degree.

After getting married, Sam felt the pressures of being able to provide for his family, so he decided to pursue additional education in business, a field he believed would lead him to a well-paying job. He did not pursue his dream of becoming a physician doing research, like Jonas Salk, because the timing did not work well with his wife's college program. His graduate school grades were excellent. His wife excelled in her studies. She completed a computer science degree and landed a job in Chicago. She expected him to find a professional job as well.

Unfortunately, Sam was not able to find a job related to his MBA when he finished his degree. He had taken this pathway to please his parents and his wife, focusing on a degree he could finish at the same time as his wife completed her studies. But his heart was not in business studies; it was in the lab.

Sam was able to find an entry-level job in a university laboratory, where he cared for the research animals. He liked this environment, but his earnings were meager. When he and his wife had children, he left his job to be a full-time parent because his wife earned much more than he did. Parenting was a very satisfying experience for him, and he felt valued.

When Sam and his wife decided to divorce, he knew he had to prepare for employment in a job that offered higher earnings than his lab job. In order to find his fit, Sam needed to use his talents in an area that matched his interests.

He decided to use his background in biology, his academic talents, and his enjoyment of a laboratory setting to return to school to prepare for a career as a biostatistician with a goal of finding employment in a medical research environment. This goal combined his interests with his desire to pursue intellectually stimulating work.

(Sam's CodeCombo is IC. See Chapter 5 to read more about ICs.)

How Lack of Understanding Hurts You

Now for the second piece of bad news: most vocational advice is not very helpful. It's not that the counselors don't have good intentions. But very few truly understand the job market. With rare exceptions, parents don't, teachers don't, and—outside of their own fields—employers don't.

And while career and guidance counselors have more training and awareness, they typically deal with hundreds of students and issues in a calendar year; therefore, they usually can't give personalized vocational guidance. In fact, most guidance counselors were not trained to help students select a career path. As a result, students who enter college without an understanding of who they are and where they fit in the world of work run into bigger and more expensive problems. Let's look at B. J., one of Tracy's students:

B. J.'S Story

B. J. was a phenomenal football player from a midsized town in the Midwest. In high school he had "hometown hero" status. Everyone in his community followed his athletic career and waited with great anticipation to see which Division I school he would attend.

B. J. did well enough in high school. But the effort he put forth in the classroom was directly related to his dream of playing college football. He didn't enjoy any of his classes. What he did like, and was very good at, was working on cars. When he wasn't at football practice or doing the schoolwork he loathed, B. J. was fixing or restoring cars for his friends and family. The front of his parents' home looked like a used car lot.

As a senior, B. J. achieved his dream of winning a football scholarship to a Big Ten university, where he was a solid player who made his family and community proud. But by the end of his first year it was clear to everyone that he didn't quite have the talent to make it to the NFL. B. J. was disappointed, but he knew that making the pros had been a long shot, so he was realistic about having to do something else for a living.

B. J. was upset about his college classes. He found them to be every bit as distasteful as his high school classes and much more difficult. He struggled to maintain a 2.0 grade point average. In his third year he chose a major, business administration, only because he had to pick something or lose his scholarship.

Meanwhile, B. J. was accumulating debt. His scholarship covered all his tuition, but he had to pay most of his own room, board, and incidental expenses.

By the middle of his third year, everything came crashing down. B. J.'s career as a football player would soon be over, he hated every one of his classes, and his debt was mounting higher every month. At the end of that semester, he dropped out, feeling frustrated, deflated, and disappointed in himself. "How did this happen?" B. J. wondered. "Somehow I got stuck sitting in stuffy classrooms, learning stuff I don't care about. And for the last two and a half years, I haven't had a moment to tinker with a single car."

(B. J.'s CodeCombo is RC. See Chapter 4 to read more about RCs.)

Misusing the Economy for Direction

Here's more bad news: because of a lack of career planning, many people look to the economy for answers, rather than to their own interests, talents, and sensibilities. They take whatever jobs are most plentiful, or the easiest to get, or the most lucrative. This creates long-term career frustration for millions of people.

Think of it this way. What if you were forced to buy a car based on what models were most widely available or what your parents thought you needed? You might be driving a minivan when you're actually interested in a sports car—or vice versa.

Speaking of driving, the labor market is what drives the nation's economy. It dictates what the jobs are, where they are, and what the market will pay. The labor market is like a gigantic switchboard with connections leading everywhere. The connections open and close as jobs become available and are eliminated.

What few people understand is that each of us has a unique connection in that giant switchboard. We can't be jammed into holes based on some generality like "the country needs more nurses" or "people with master's degrees make more money"—not if we're going to perform at our best, get the most satisfaction from our work, and contribute the most to our organizations and the world.

Let's take a closer look at these generalizations for a moment and see how easily they can lead people astray.

The country needs more nurses. It's true; the United States *does* need more nurses. But if your natural interests and talents have nothing to do with healthcare, what sense does it make to earn a nursing degree—especially if it leads to a job you won't enjoy and won't be especially good at? Yet lots of people do exactly this—and lots of others counsel them to do it—simply because nursing jobs pay well and are plentiful.

People with master's degrees make more money. In general, it's true that the more education you have, the more money you will earn. But we all know loads of exceptions. Common sense tells us that someone with an MA in art history or philosophy will usually earn less than a skilled welder who completed a nine-month technical training program, or an assertive and savvy marketer with a high school diploma.

Yet it's generalities like these that cause most Americans to follow one of three potentially disastrous career paths:

1. **They go to college based mostly on the idea that a college degree will help them earn more money and get a better job.** Often encouraged by their parents, teachers, friends, and family, they focus their efforts on saving for college, getting into college, and securing financial aid for college. Meanwhile, they spend little or no time considering what their interests are and how those might relate to the world of work, or what education they'll actually need to match the two.

2. **They choose a career based on trial and error.** They find a place to live—or they stay in the town where they grew up—and get a job that uses some of their abilities. If it works out reasonably well, they try to get promoted; if it doesn't, they move on to something else. They wander through the labor market without a plan.

3. **They focus on money, job security, or both—completely ignoring their own interests, happiness, and satisfaction.** There's nothing wrong with doing something temporarily just for the money—but if you do it year after year for forty hours a week, you're going to suffer enormously.

All right, enough of the bad news. You now know the challenges. Are you ready for the solution? Here is the GOOD NEWS!

Let *CareerCode* Be Your Guide

CareerCode can be your map. Even if you've already wandered the roads of unsatisfying careers for years, as Jade did (whose CodeCombo is AR; see Chapter 6 to read more about ARs), it's not too late for you to find a new direction.

These cutting-edge concepts can help you to...

- avoid years of painful trial and error working at jobs that don't suit you.
- save thousands—even tens of thousands—of dollars that you might otherwise spend on inappropriate or unnecessary education.
- quickly learn which jobs and fields will most likely bring you happiness and success—and which ones will likely lead to misery.
- pinpoint the education you need for the careers that best suit you.
- focus your efforts on those jobs where you can attain the greatest satisfaction and success.
- do a reality check to make sure you are on the right path.
- lose your uncertainty and confusion, and find confidence and clarity.
- build your career—and your personal and professional success—in a faster, more focused, and vastly more effective way.

But that's not all. Once you understand how Career-Code works, you'll be able to apply it in dozens of practical ways. You'll better understand how other people think, what motivates them, how to get along with them, how to please and impress them, and how to solve or prevent conflicts.

The lessons of *CareerCode* can help you create better relationships with your friends, your family, and people you meet for the first time. We're not exaggerating to say that *CareerCode* will make you more effective in all your relationships and give you a stronger sense of self and a more positive and empowered outlook on life.

There's yet another benefit to *CareerCode*: no longer will your parent, spouse, partner, sibling, or boss be able to pressure you to make an unwise career move. If you know your CareerCode, you will be in a position to evaluate ideas and suggestions realistically. If they don't make sense to you, show others the pages of this book that describe your Code-Combo. You may see a light bulb appear above their heads.

As it was for our students and clients, *CareerCode* can be the key to a personal revolution. People are happiest when they feel a strong connection to their purpose in life—when they can go home after their workday is finished and feel proud of what they do for a living, when they feel they are making a difference, or when they simply feel they're doing something exciting or fun.

Your key to a happy and successful future is only a few pages away. It rests with your CareerCode. Turn the page, and let's get started.

CHAPTER 3

Cracking Your Code

You're now ready to discover your own personalized Career-Code. As you go through this process, please keep a few things in mind:

- These codes help describe your interests, passions, and motivations. They are *not* a comprehensive personality evaluation.
- No one CareerCode is better (or worse) than any other.
- CareerCodes don't discriminate based on culture, sex, race, age, religion, or anything else.
- Your CareerCode will reveal not only what you like and are interested in but what you *don't* like. This will be some of the most valuable information you can have when choosing a job or career.
- Your CareerCode may change a bit over time. While big upheavals in your codes are very un-

likely, even over years or decades, small changes (like moving from SE to ES) are not uncommon.

- The CareerCode process has been carefully developed, tested, and refined for years. We know from extensive testing that it works extremely well for almost everyone who uses it. However, like all systems created by human beings, Career-Code isn't 100 percent perfect—so please don't expect it to be.

The Interest Codes and You

There are six basic Interest Codes. Each describes a set of interests, likes, dislikes, and attitudes toward work environments. Remember, there are no bad or good Interest Codes; they are descriptions, not judgments.

Each of us has a little bit of all six Interest Codes, and typically we each have two or three Interest Codes that are stronger than others. The process you're about to follow will enable you to notice the influence each of these six codes has on your preferences and environmental gratification.

The six Interest Codes are:

- Realistic (R)
- Investigative (I)
- Artistic (A)
- Social (S)
- Enterprising (E)
- Conventional (C)

R Realistic

Realistic people have athletic or mechanical ability (or both) and prefer to work with objects, machines, tools, plants, or animals. They are often practical, concrete, conservative, and systematic. Their comments are frank and straightforward, though their manner is often reserved. They like their accomplishments to be tangible and measurable. Their hobbies include fixing things, playing sports, attending races, using tools, gardening or farming, building structures, and working on vehicles. Realistic people like to be outdoors, and they are generally adventuresome. Their preferred vacation destinations include parks, wilderness settings, and nature tours where interaction with others is limited.

I Investigative

Investigative people like to observe, learn, research, analyze, evaluate, and solve problems. They are often inquisitive, analytical, precise, scientific, independent, introspective, logical, and curious. Their hobbies and interests include thinking abstractly, solving math problems, reading scientific theories, analyzing data, researching, and exploring ideas. They enjoy being challenged and working independently. They like to plan vacations with independent activities such as visiting museums and historical sites, or they like to simply find a place to catch up on their reading.

A Artistic

Artistic people are innovative, intuitive, and talented. They enjoy working in unstructured settings where they can use their imagination and creativity. They are often expressive, idealistic, sensitive, impulsive, and open. They can be complicated and, surprisingly, are often conventional. Their hobbies and interests include any or all of the arts: sketching, drawing, painting, playing a musical instrument, singing, listening to music, writing, reading, designing things (especially clothing and interior spaces), and attending concerts, plays, and art exhibits. Their ideal vacation destinations are big cities where they can be surrounded by the arts, boutique shops, and many aesthetic experiences.

S Social

Social people enjoy enlightening, informing, helping, training, healing, and working with others. They are often friendly, helpful, insightful, nurturing, patient, persuasive, understanding, cooperative, empathetic, responsible, kind, and skillful with words. Their hobbies and interests include volunteer activities where they can help others, especially the young, the old, and the disadvantaged. They like to lead group discussions, assist with the social aspects of fundraising, and work on teams that improve the social welfare of a community. When on vacation, they are less concerned with the destination than with being able to interact with good friends and family members.

E Enterprising

Enterprising people like to influence, persuade, lead, and manage others in order to make money or achieve organizational goals. They are frequently assertive, persuasive, self-confident, impulsive, popular, talkative, extroverted, dominant, enthusiastic, adventurous, and optimistic. Their interests and hobbies include initiating projects or activities, making deals, selling and promoting ideas, joining business groups, networking with important people, running for elected office, and competing for leadership awards. When on vacation, they like being among movers and shakers—particularly in luxury surroundings where they can be seen by others. Enterprising people rarely leave their cell phones behind.

C Conventional

Conventional people enjoy working with data or things while performing organized activities and doing detailed tasks. They are dependable, methodical, efficient, practical, accurate, systematic, structured, polite, reliable, and persistent. They are good at keeping records, making schedules, following budgets, and organizing environments. They often have collections (stamps, coins, posters, etc.) and enjoy creating things that require precision, such as cabinetmaking, quilts, or needlepoint. On vacation they like taking structured tours led by people who can provide detailed information about their surroundings. They want to know the schedule.

In almost everyone, two Interest Codes are more prominent than the others; these are the ones that exert the strongest influence on an individual. As you'll see, this two-letter CodeCombo yields very specific and useful results. Adding a third code enables you to further refine the CodeCombo and CareerCode results.

For example, the basic Interest Code for 90 percent of all educators begins with S, or Social. But a music teacher, a business skills teacher, and an industrial arts teacher have very different specializations and work environments, so it's no surprise that they have different CodeCombos. (Think of the educators you have known. Are all of them alike? Of course not.)

Let's look at how the CodeCombo helps define some of the different education-related specialties:

- SA (Social/Artistic): music, art, English, and speech teachers
- SE (Social/Enterprising): school counselors
- SI (Social/Investigative): science and math teachers
- SR (Social/Realistic): physical education and industrial arts teachers
- SC (Social/Conventional): business skills and home economics teachers

These CodeCombos also apply to activities outside of formal classes. SAs (English, speech, art, and music teachers) often sponsor the student newspaper, the yearbook, and the debate teams. A school counselor (probably an SE) might be involved with the student council. Many physical education teachers (usually SRs) are also coaches.

Now let's look at the code differentiation process again, this time for lawyers. We usually think of lawyers as people who argue cases in a courtroom, because that's what we see in movies and TV shows. But, in fact, the legal profession is extremely diverse. A patent attorney has a very different job from one who specializes in family law. Job tasks for a labor relations attorney are not the same as those of a corporate lawyer; in fact, sometimes they face off against each other. An intellectual property lawyer, who needs to prepare technical paperwork, may have an engineering degree. While all lawyers receive similar training, their individual CodeCombos determine which legal specialties might best suit them. For example:

- Investigative/Enterprising (IE): patent lawyers
- Enterprising/Social (ES): family law attorneys
- Enterprising/Realistic (ER): labor relations lawyers, real estate attorneys
- Enterprising/Conventional (EC): corporate lawyers
- Enterprising/Artistic (EA): trial lawyers, lobbyists

Note that not all lawyers share the same one-letter Interest Code. Although most lawyers are Es, a few are IEs. (It's rare, however, for a happy and successful lawyer not to have an E as part of his or her two-letter CodeCombo.)

Your Personalized Ranking

On the next few pages you'll see short descriptions of the six Interest Codes. Each probably describes at least one or two things which appeal to you. Some describe you better than others, although none probably describes you perfectly.

Read all six Interest Code descriptions carefully. (It's okay to go back and reread any of them at any time.)

When you're done reading, rank all six Interest Codes in Figure 1, *in the order in which they best describe you.* For example, if Social (S) describes you best, Artistic (A) second best, Conventional (C) third best, Investigative (I) fourth, Realistic (R) fifth, and Enterprising (E) least of all, your ranking will look like this:

1. S
2. A
3. C
4. I
5. R
6. E

Figure 1

In this example, your first letter (S) is your basic Interest Code. Your first two letters, in order—in this case, SA—is your CodeCombo. All six letters in order—SACIRE—is your CareerCode.

If this were your CodeCombo, you would now turn to Chapter 7 to read about the Social/Artistic (SA) CodeCombo in more detail. The mirror image of your CodeCombo—the same two letters, but reversed—may also describe you fairly or very well. So after you've read about the Social/Artistic (SA) CodeCombo, turn to Chapter 6 and read about the Artistic/Social (AS) CodeCombo, and see how the SA and AS compare. After you've selected your own CodeCombo, try this mirroring process using your two-letter CodeCombo.

When you're done reading and thinking about the six Interest Codes, rank the six codes in the box below, starting with your strongest code, followed by the second strongest, and continuing until you have rank-ordered all six codes. (The same letter will appear as #1 in all three columns. Similarly, the same letter will appear in the #2 position in both the center and right-hand columns.)

Your Interest Code	Your CodeCombo	Your CareerCode
1. _____	1. _____	1. _____
	2. _____	2. _____
		3. _____
		4. _____
		5. _____
		6. _____

Congratulations! You've come up with your own Interest Code, CodeCombo, and CareerCode. You now have everything you need to unlock a wealth of information about yourself, your interests, and your future happiness and success.

Before moving ahead, you may find it worthwhile to identify Interest Codes, CodeCombos, and CareerCodes for other important people in your life, including friends and family. This will help you understand individual similarities and differences. Even if you do not get all the codes exactly right, engaging in this exercise will help you learn to apply CareerCode to the people you encounter. The following pages contain charts for you to fill out; take a stab by entering the codes of the most significant people in your life, and then you will be prepared to read their CodeCombo descriptions to see if they fit .

Below are eight charts for you to fill out for the significant people in your life, including parents, stepparents, spouse, partner, siblings, children, and close friends. At the top of each chart, write the name of the person, and then fill in the codes.

Codes for: _____

Interest Code	CodeCombo	CareerCode
1. _____	1. _____	1. _____
	2. _____	2. _____
		3. _____
		4. _____
		5. _____
		6. _____

Codes for: _____

Interest Code	CodeCombo	CareerCode
1. _____	1. _____	1. _____
	2. _____	2. _____
		3. _____
		4. _____
		5. _____
		6. _____

Codes for: _____

Interest Code	CodeCombo	CareerCode
1. _____	1. _____	1. _____
	2. _____	2. _____
		3. _____
		4. _____
		5. _____
		6. _____

Codes for: _____

Interest Code	CodeCombo	CareerCode
1. _____	1. _____	1. _____
	2. _____	2. _____
		3. _____
		4. _____
		5. _____
		6. _____

Codes for: _____

Interest Code	CodeCombo	CareerCode
1. _____	1. _____	1. _____
	2. _____	2. _____
		3. _____
		4. _____
		5. _____
		6. _____

Codes for: _____

Interest Code	CodeCombo	CareerCode
1. _____	1. _____	1. _____
	2. _____	2. _____
		3. _____
		4. _____
		5. _____
		6. _____

Codes for: _____

Interest Code	CodeCombo	CareerCode
1. _____	1. _____	1. _____
	2. _____	2. _____
		3. _____
		4. _____
		5. _____
		6. _____

Codes for: _____

Interest Code	CodeCombo	CareerCode
1. _____	1. _____	1. _____
	2. _____	2. _____
		3. _____
		4. _____
		5. _____
		6. _____

As you read through the next six chapters, which describe each Interest Code and CodeCombo in more detail, you might want to come back to this section and decide if you want to make any changes to the codes you have assigned to your family and friends. You may also want to share this book with them, so they can learn more about the codes, take the test, and develop insights about CareerCodes.

CHAPTER 4

Realistic (R): The Doers

There are people who make the world work. They build the houses we live in. When we have a problem with the plumbing or want a new deck built, we call them. They repair our transmissions and fix our shoes. They restore the fallen power lines after thunderstorms; and, for that matter, they install the storm sewers that carry the rain away. When we go out to eat at a nice restaurant, they are probably the ones who built the restaurant, who cooked the meal we eat, and who grew the grapes to make the wine we drink.

They are the engineers, the gardeners, the builders, the road crew workers, the farmers, the cooks, the tailors, and the mechanics. The people described by these job titles are people whose primary Interest Code is R, or Realistic.

But the R code may also apply to people who are working in a field that doesn't fit them. Maybe it's the man who works behind the counter at the bank, daydreaming about getting home to work on the next step in the backyard landscaping project or tinker with the used bike from the yard sale. Maybe it's the woman who went to college and majored in management—because, you know, she had to pick *something*—and feeling empty most of the time even if her bank account isn't. Maybe it's the high school senior who loved working for his uncle's landscaping company over the summer but has no idea how that translates into a career choice that will satisfy Mom and Dad.

In general, if you like to work with your hands, or if you believe that sore muscles at the end of the day are a sign of a job well done, or if you've always been the first of your peers to reach the gym, you have prominent R traits.

If your first code is R, then you are very likely…

- practical
- hands-on
- structured
- athletic
- reserved
- hardworking

The R Interest Style

Does this sound like you? You like to tinker with, build, maintain, mend, and repair things in your environment. Maybe you're out working in your yard the minute you have free time, building a stone path or working on flowerbeds that are the envy of the neighborhood.

Perhaps the garage is your habitat. Ever since you were a kid, you had a natural talent for figuring out how things worked, and now you apply that ability to working on your car or building a basketball hoop for the kids. In high school, you snoozed through English class but perked right up when it was time for industrial technology.

Whether it's fixing cars, building furniture, knitting, or even cooking, you like hands-on work that produces results you can see and something you can use. When you think about what you'd love to do for a living, it probably involves making something or figuring out how to make something work—something big like houses or bridges, or something small like microchips or jewelry.

In general, R's dislike change. They don't mind working the same hours every day. They like their life and work to be stable, steady, and predictable.

How R's Can Get in Trouble

R's view the world in terms of black and white, right and wrong. Consequently, they have strong opinions and can be stubborn about them. They can get themselves into trouble when they refuse to bend.

R's may know how something works, but they may not want to take the time to explain the process to others. They learn their jobs by doing, not by talking. An R car mechanic or surgeon may be very talented, and may consistently do great work, but they don't want to comment or talk about it; they just want to do it. When R's need to communicate with someone, they'll usually do so in only a few concise words, often with little empathy. This does not win them friends.

Education for R's

R's usually learn on the job or through a combination of specialized training and on-the-job experience. R's therefore spend less time in school and more time working to hone their skills than any other Interest Code.

Many R's tell us that they did not enjoy classroom study, which was often difficult, frustrating, and boring. Most R's don't want to sit at a desk; they learn best by doing.

Most R jobs require specialized training such as hands-on trade and technical programs. Because these typically last six months to two years—and because some of these programs are offered to high school students—R's usually enter the workforce fairly early. One common exception, however, are engineering jobs, which require at least a bachelor's degree and in some cases graduate work.

R CodeCombos

- RI: The Engineer
- RA: The Crafter
- RS: The Attendant
- RE: The Sergeant
- RC: The Technician

RI Realistic/Investigative: The Engineer

The RI credo: *I can build a better mousetrap.*

If you're Realistic/Investigative (RI), you're probably…

- *methodical.* When you buy a new appliance, you read warnings in the instruction manual before turning it on.
- *diligent.* You might work longer hours than anyone else on your block.
- *strict.* The phrase "close enough" isn't in your vocabulary.
- *thrifty.* You're a penny pincher and proud of it.
- *introverted.* Big social gatherings give you the jitters.
- *critical.* Work that doesn't meet your standards really gets on your nerves.
- *rational.* No sob stories for you—just the cold, hard facts.
- *hard on yourself.* You're your own toughest critic.
- *technology oriented.* You love new tools and gadgets. The well-designed ones impress you; the bad ones tick you off.

The RI Brain

In order to be truly satisfied with a job, an RI needs the opportunity to find solutions, explore new territory, and use specialized training or expertise to do things other people can only dream about. The RI's primary urge is to innovate and find ingenious ways to make things work.

If you're an RI, you will probably like working with scientific knowledge and its technical applications. You have a knack for solving problems. Even in your day-to-day life, you enjoy solving problems; your highly developed sense of logic makes Sudoku puzzles a piece of cake, and you're the one who can walk into a situation and point out the obvious problem nobody else has noticed. For example: "The table isn't wobbling because the legs are loose. It's because the floor isn't level."

You take your work seriously and prefer to focus on specific, productive tasks. You are an innovator and a problem solver, and you are excited by new and unusual tasks. You are project oriented from beginning to end, and you can't relax until you finish what you start.

You like to earn money, but you don't necessarily enjoy spending it. Money is a measure of your worth, however, and since you feel you're capable of things most other people aren't, you believe you're worth a good deal of it.

You don't like to dress up for work. You prefer to wear the most casual things you can find in your closet.

How RI's Relate to Others

A classic RI likes to work with people who are prepared. If this is your CodeCombo, nothing irks you more than a coworker or a classmate who shows up and says, "I'm sorry, but my hard drive died last night and took my presentation with it."

In fact, you really don't like doing things in groups, whether it's your lab in biology class or your project group at work. You'd much rather plug away on a project independently.

If you're stuck with a manager, supervisor, or teacher who doesn't "get it" or seems to have a lower IQ than you, you'll be miserable.

You don't have a lot of patience with people. When you explain something, you expect your pupil to understand the first time around.

You're not especially interested in networking, hobnobbing, going to cocktail parties, or building relationships. If someone wants to talk to you, they can leave a message on your voice mail; you will try to get back to them when you have the time. Truth be told, you would prefer someone take care of the more frivolous details, such as the social calendar, gift buying, and doing the laundry, because slogging through those kinds of tasks seems like the worst kind of chore.

The Miscast RI

The RI's primary drive is to gather specialized information and use it to solve problems, preferably in ways that nobody else has come up with. Making things work is a matter of pride, and it's also a valuable contribution—to the world, or just the neighborhood. Absent this opportunity, RIs can feel restless and stifled.

Working in a hands-on capacity is important to the RI, thanks to the dominant Realistic CareerCode, but simply doing physical labor may not be enough to truly satisfy an

RI, because the Investigative aspect requires the opportunity to explore and innovate. An RI who's stuck in a data entry job might feel that digging ditches would be more rewarding than sitting at a keyboard all day—and that may actually be true. But really, *designing* the county's drainage ditch system would be a far better fit.

Picture Yourself as an Engineer

Engineers can work in dozens of different fields with at least as many specialties. But they have many things in common, foremost of which is their intense involvement in science, technology, or mathematics and their ability to apply their knowledge to solve problems.

As an engineer, your computer is your best friend. You most likely have a laptop with a huge memory, so you can use it in your home office as well. It will probably have a large screen for modeling.

You'll use computers to design products, devices, public works, or systems; to simulate how they operate; and to follow the process through production and quality control. If you're a biomedical engineer, you may help design a new kind of drug-coated stent for heart patients; as a civil engineer, you might work on a multimillion-dollar freeway tunnel; as an electronics engineer, you might design an MP3 player or a microwave.

You'll likely have a large desk to house your computer, all your work materials, and lots of relevant reference books. These will need to be close at hand so you can easily research something, then keep moving forward with your project.

Regardless of your specialty, you'll probably work in an

office or in a lab, and you might travel frequently to monitor projects in progress or confer with other specialists. Your work will be centered on whatever the latest project is, and each new project to come along will bring its own set of unique challenges. If you're an RI, these challenges are invigorating, and your drive to find innovative solutions keeps you motivated.

Successful efforts are supremely satisfying. You'll feel stimulated by your work and proud of your ability to take theoretical knowledge and turn it into real things that people use, and maybe even things that will change the world.

RI Education Requirements

RI jobs require high aptitude in science and math. RI career paths normally require at least a bachelor's degree. Many careers in specialized fields require a master's degree.

RI Job Opportunities

These are abundant. In fact, most RI's needn't be concerned about whether they will get a job when they finish their training. Instead, the real challenge for the RI is choosing a specialization. This choice is important for three reasons: First, some specializations pay much better than others. Second, some specialties have more jobs than others, especially in certain locales. And third, for RIs, the path to higher earnings won't involve going into management or supervision, which RIs loathe—it will be through developing specialized expertise.

Some RI jobs, such as chemical or mechanical engineering, are plentiful and found almost everywhere. An RI interested in aeronautical engineering will need to locate on the West Coast, as there are far fewer jobs elsewhere. An RI interested in petroleum engineering will probably need to live near oil fields or refineries.

RI Celebrity

Neil Armstrong, aeronautical engineer and astronaut
Neil Armstrong is an RI. He is persistent, determined, and analytical. Armstrong earned a BS in aeronautical engineering from Purdue University in 1955 and a Master of Science degree in aerospace engineering from the University of Southern California. He is an aviator, test pilot, and astronaut.

> *I believe every human has a finite number of heartbeats.*
> *I don't intend to waste any of mine.*
>
> —Neil Armstrong

RA Realistic/Artistic: The Crafter

The RA credo: *Another person's junk is my treasure.*

If you're Realistic/Artistic (RA), you're probably...

- *project focused.* You're already planning your next project before the current one ends.
- *into patterns.* A perfectly designed mosaic is a beautiful thing.

- *interested in R & R.* To you, this means "restoration and repair." You can easily spend hours at your workbench.
- *a perfectionist.* You will nitpick your own work, often noticing things others would never see.
- *introverted.* You like your own company just fine, thank you.
- *self-reliant.* You don't like being told what to do, and you don't like having to tell others, either.
- *minimalist.* You don't require a lot of expensive possessions to be happy, but you do need your projects.
- *tenacious.* You'll spend hours performing repetitive tasks in order to attain perfection.
- *resourceful.* Who said that Aunt Edna's old antique dresser needed to go? You can turn it into something Pottery Barn would be proud to sell for big bucks.

The RA Brain

An RA is happiest when pursuing creative projects—but not the kind of creative projects you're probably going to encounter in a trip to an art museum or at a poetry reading. The typical RA would rather modify a motorcycle than write a ballad.

The RA brain is good at sizing things up spatially and planning how to turn one thing into something else, whether it's transforming a stack of boards into a bookshelf or converting a stack of vegetables into a culinary delight.

If you're an RA, you're probably patient and willing to do painstaking work to get something right. As a kid, maybe you were the one who assembled the perfectly symmetrical gingerbread house while your siblings or classmates were busy eating the frosting. Even as an adult, the prospect of creating something that's just right really gets your perfectionist motor running. If your job doesn't give you the opportunity to create and work with your hands, maybe you'll find other outlets, such as helping your kids with their Pinewood Derby cars or assembling quilts with painstaking detail.

Maybe these traits sound like you: You love to scavenge for useful items at garage sales and auctions. You hesitate to buy anything new, because you know it's so much cheaper and more original to get a used item and restore it. You enjoy developing a niche or a specialty, either as a profession or as a hobby, and when others ask you about it, you're delighted to talk to them about it for as long as they'll listen.

You like to collect things such as antique cars, trains, or dolls. Let's face it, eBay was a dream come true for you. Everyone thinks your life and possessions are disorderly and chaotic. But if they ask you to find something in your stash, you know exactly where it is.

How RA's Relate to Others

You enjoy getting things done alone. In fact, you thrive on autonomy or finding a valuable gadget or knickknack when the opportunity presents.

It is difficult for you to trust others to complete a project to your high standards. You can be fairly opinionated and critical about the work of others, especially if you're collaborating with them—or have to clean up (or fix) their messes.

Whether or not your paying job gives you an outlet for your desire to create, you are happiest when you get a chance to work on projects. Because you prefer being alone—or with a few, very close friends or family members—others may describe you as a homebody. To you, social climbing is a complete waste of time.

The Miscast RA

If you're an RA and you're stuck in a career that doesn't provide the satisfaction of getting lost in projects, using your hands, and creating things that serve an important function or brighten up the world, you will probably be miserable unless the impulse to create can be channeled into a productive hobby. As dissatisfaction at work increases, the more wrapped up in the hobby you are likely to become. This is because RA's don't feel useful unless they are creating something tangible and doing it well. Some RA's might be satisfied enough, even when they're miscast in their job, if they can set up a woodshop in the garage or focus their creative energy on crafts around the house, but they probably won't feel totally fulfilled unless they can find ways to do those kinds of projects in their professional life.

If you feel much more pride when you put a perfect coat of paint on the kitchen walls than you do when you get a good performance review at work, you might be a miscast RA. If you're staring at the clock all afternoon on Friday, thinking about what you need to get from the hardware store for your weekend projects, you'd probably be happier at a job that lets your Realistic and Artistic sides shine.

Picture Yourself as an Artisan

From what we've described, you can probably see that an RA is a natural fit for a job that involves building things, fixing things, or otherwise tinkering. Such a person might work behind the counter of a jewelry shop fixing watches or necklaces. Maybe your cup of tea would be starting your own business making things out of wood and selling them at craft markets.

An RA also might work in a noisy shop, filled with buzzing machines, where people are creating things out of iron or building cabinets that will be shipped off to home-improvement retailers.

Regardless of your specialty, your focus is building, restoring, and repairing things. You're able to do repairs and restorations that others don't have the talent or patience for, and that ability fills you with confidence.

Your shop or workbench is the center of your universe. Whether you work for yourself or someone else, you absolutely need your own space or bench or work area and your own tools or utensils.

When you're working on a project, you become completely lost in it. Sometimes you completely lose track of time—which is totally fine with you. And you can get irritable if someone interrupts your work.

Because you are sometimes more interested in the act of crafting than in selling your work, you may find projects stacking up in your workshop. Your shop may be dirty and disorderly, with piles of tools and odds and ends. But that's okay; you are used to working in disarray. What's most important is having enough space for your projects and tools.

RA Education Requirements

Most RA jobs require technical training—for example, in a welding program or a culinary school. (The prospect of such training may make some RA's—especially those with a strong artistic bent—bristle a bit.) Some require on-the-job training through an internship or apprenticeship. Although a handful of RA fields, such as art restoration, may require a bachelor's degree, the great majority of them do not. However, many RA jobs do require innate artistic talent.

Some RA jobs—furniture design and Japanese cooking, for example—are so specialized that training programs may be available in only a handful of locations.

RA Job Opportunities

Unfortunately, RA jobs are not plentiful. Advances in technology have made the market for many of the old-school RA jobs, such as cobblers, tailors, and other skilled tradespeople, much smaller.

Nevertheless, some solid RA career paths remain. These include cabinetmaking, sign painting, and floral design (though in some locations it's tough to find steady work). Some of the best options for RA's are culinary jobs—pastry chef, cake decorator, and sous-chef.

In rural areas and many small towns, there are few or no RA jobs. Many RA's who live in these places set up their own small business or choose to work in careers that don't especially interest them and express their RA-ness in projects they do in their spare time. One good compromise for many of these RA's is to take AR jobs, which are far more plentiful.

RA Celebrity

Carey Hart, freestyle motocrosser, entrepreneur, and reality TV star

Carey Hart is an RA. He is daring, visceral, and edgy. Hart is a freestyle motocross racer and co-owner of Hart and Huntington Tattoos, one of the most famous places in the world to get "inked," with shops at the Palms and Hard Rock casinos in Las Vegas. The A&E network followed him and the workings of the shop in the reality show *Inked*.

> *Honestly, it started off as a novelty. I just had this itch to open a tattoo shop. It wasn't going to be [anything] really crazy, but I just went out there with really good artists to do something kind of cool and unique.*
>
> —Carey Hart

 ## Realistic/Social: The Attendant

The RS credo: *How can I be of service?*

If you're Realistic/Social (RS), you're probably...

- *dependable.* Everyone trusts you to come through for them—and you do.

- *fraternal.* You still keep in touch with your elementary school classmates.
- *busy.* If you aren't fixing something, you're probably talking to someone.
- *a problem solver.* You genuinely want to lend a hand and find a solution—and you're usually successful.
- *a facilitator.* You take pride in being the link between people with differing interests and needs.
- *community oriented.* You create a sense of community just by showing up.
- *athletic.* You love to play sports for both the physical activity and the sense of camaraderie.
- *helpful.* You aim to please.
- *practical.* You're much less concerned with theories and big ideas than you are with what works.
- *hands on.* You'll never be seen standing around, letting others do the work.
- *responsive.* You take care of people and do what's needed.

The RS Brain

An RS is, above all, hands-on and helpful. An RS will not stand around and watch as somebody else does the work. RS's are always thinking of how to help family, friends, and co-workers get things done, not just because they feel obligated, but because they truly believe it's the right thing to do—and it makes them feel good about themselves and the world.

Like the other R CodeCombos, those who best fit the RS mold are happiest in environments that are mechanical, industrial, or highly physical. But if you're an RS, unlike most of the other R CodeCombos, you also need more interaction with other people (or, in some cases, with animals) while you provide a service.

You feel pleased and empowered when people ask you to help them figure something out, and you're happy when a project is completed successfully and everyone is satisfied. Maybe you get this feeling at work when you help customers or clients find the help they need when nobody else could; or it may be at home, when you planned the family vacation and made it fun for everybody; or it could be in your social life, when you were asked to help a friend paint the house and showed up with supplies to donate, drinks to share, and a community-minded attitude that got the entire group going.

In your ideal job, having a desk isn't important to you. Neither is a computer. You'd probably rather use your phone, which is much more personal and immediate. You want to be making things happen and connecting with your coworkers and customers, not sitting in a cubicle cut off from the rest of the world.

If you're like most RS's, you love caring for animals. Thus, you might make a great animal control officer, veterinary technician, or animal trainer.

As an RS, you don't necessarily need to be solving world hunger to feel like you're making a difference. You may be happy driving a delivery van or truck, a hotel or airport shuttle, a charter bus, or a school bus. Those kinds of jobs allow you to interact with a wide variety of people every day and know that you are helping by providing an important service.

If you're an RS, you're not all that hard to please; you're basically pretty happy as long as you're helping others and able to have time for your family, friends, and community activities.

How RS's Relate to Others

Because you are social, having coworkers and getting along with them are important to you. You are likely to befriend your coworkers, both inside and outside of the workplace. You also like knowing that you have a strong network of friends, colleagues, former coworkers, and schoolmates to draw on. You're the kind of person who always seems to have a friend of a friend who can help with almost any situation.

Because you're naturally likable, you probably get along well with your superior, your manager, your coworkers, the office assistants, the cleaning crew, and just about everyone else you come across. Your presence creates a team spirit at work because you naturally work for the common good.

When it comes to getting things done as part of a group, or on behalf of one, you consider this your time to shine. You're likely to organize the company softball team or the barbecue. In school, you were the one everybody wanted in their study team or lab group. In those kinds of situations, you're good at making everybody feel welcome, encouraging everyone to participate, and nudging the group toward its goals.

The Miscast RS

As you might imagine, an RS's worst nightmare would be working alone, working in a capacity that doesn't seem to have tangible results to help people, or both. If you're an RS, cleaning offices after everybody's gone home is not for you. Neither is being a park ranger, stationed in the middle of nowhere with few people or even animals in sight. Filing paperwork or organizing library books is probably not your thing. In those situations, an RS can feel like work is pretty pointless and wind up longing for more connection and sense of purpose. An RS also shares the dominant Realistic Interest Code with the other R CodeCombos, which means a job that doesn't have a hands-on component that involves producing or fixing something would be a mismatch.

However, one unique characteristic of people with the RS CodeCombo is that as long as they are able to feel helpful to people, and have at least some coworkers around to chat with and feel good about, they can be relatively happy in a wide variety of jobs. Maybe filing paperwork wouldn't be so bad if you could do it in an office with three or four other people who worked as a team, and you could feel you were a key part of keeping the office running smoothly.

Picture Yourself as a Coach Driver

You work for a charter bus company that provides coach transportation services for tour groups, community organizations, and business groups. Your job is to serve traveling customers and transport them to sporting events, casinos, business meetings, or scenic tours. You handle customer concerns and operate the bus in a professional manner. You maintain good communication with riders and the tour director to coordinate schedules and ensure quality services. You like the combination of being physically active while also being able to interact with people. You like to be helpful and solve problems for riders and management. You enjoy having repeat customers, because that means you have built and maintained a good relationship with them. You love it when your customers become friends.

You can be found where people congregate. Where you won't be found is in a cubicle or a tucked-away office. You hate to be tied down and enjoy being out and about. You move easily between indoor and outdoor environments. You are interested in being where you are most needed and where you have an opportunity to visit with others.

You like to be involved in your community. You're delighted when the Lions Club recognizes you for being an outstanding community member—yet you were really just being yourself.

RS Education Requirements

Most RS's learn their trades through on-the-job experience or from mentors; there are very few formal educational programs for RS jobs. (Exceptions include training for veterinary technicians or police academy instructors; these typically require one to two years of training at a technical college.) In some cases, RS's go to technical school to learn trades such as printing or auto mechanics but find ways to make those jobs relationship oriented through providing customer service activities.

RS Job Opportunities

RS's can be happy in many technical trades, so long as they find ways to interact with customers. Often this means finding positions such as a customer service advisor in an auto repair shop or client advisor in a print shop. Thus RS's have job options almost anywhere in the country, in both rural and metropolitan areas.

RS's generally have little trouble getting jobs because of their networks of friends and acquaintances. Also, most employers are happy to hire RSs because they are pleasant to be around and usually very team oriented.

RS Celebrity

Andy Griffith, actor and star of *The Andy Griffith Show*
The character, Andy Taylor is an RS. He is strong, courageous, and sincere. While Andy Griffith had many notable roles in his career, he is most famous for starring on *The Andy Griffith Show*, a show that took place in the fictional town of Mayberry, North Carolina, where he played Andy Taylor, a widower and single father who was the town sheriff and sage.

Andy Taylor also fits an RS persona with his friendly demeanor and the way he's always available to help out his neighbors and community. He takes his son fishing and leads the local Boy Scout troop.

When a man carries a gun all the time, the respect he thinks he's getting might really be fear. So I don't carry a gun because I don't want the people of Mayberry to fear a gun. I'd rather they respect me.

—Andy Taylor

RE Realistic/Enterprising: The Sergeant

The RE credo: *Get it done!*

If you're Realistic/Enterprising (RE), you're probably...

- *a natural supervisor.* You love being in charge.
- *dependable.* You do what you say you'll do.
- *a black-and-white thinker.* It's yes or no, stop or go. You rarely see gray areas.
- *opinionated.* You know when you're right, which is almost always.
- *aggressive.* When you want something done, you speak right up.
- *autocratic.* It's your way or the highway. It's not always pretty, but it gets things done.
- *a self-starter.* You're a doer, and you always have a clear agenda.
- *a motivator.* You move and shake others.
- *determined.* You're going to get what you want, one way or another.
- *stubborn.* You refuse to back down. Most of the time, it works, and you get your way more often than not.
- *a hard worker.* No afternoon snoozes for you. There's always more to do.
- *temperamental.* You were born with a short fuse.

The RE Brain

If you're an RE, you're an alpha dog through and through. You have an assertive, take-charge style, and you're after results in everything you do.

It comes naturally for you to enforce the rules and expect others to follow them. You are used to getting your way. You get frustrated when others don't do their best or don't do a job right, because you know things don't get done if slackers are involved.

In your personal and professional lives, you are willing to carry a big load and assume big risks if the situation warrants. Some extreme REs go a step further in their risk taking, embracing danger and living on the edge.

You are good at forming a quick opinion about how things should be done, and you're not shy about expressing it. You don't see the point in discussing it when there's an obvious solution and work to be done. When you were a kid and your friends were debating how to get the Frisbee off the roof, you ignored them, climbed up a tree, and shimmied across a limb onto the roof to retrieve it. When the basement flooded after a thunderstorm, you didn't need to call an expert or wait around for somebody to help: you started issuing instructions and taking care of the situation yourself.

You're not what would be called a social climber, but you are interested in rising to the top. Partly this is because it will please your ego, and partly it's because you just think things will get done better if you are in charge. At work, you are very aware of promotional opportunities, and you will strategize and do whatever you can to obtain the best possible position.

Many RE's would rather be the first officer of a small plane than the second officer of a large one. It may be lonely at the top, but that's the only place you want to be.

How RE's Relate to Others

You may be respected by your coworkers, but you aren't necessarily liked, because your tendency to take charge can come off as abrasive. That's okay with you. You're not at work to win a popularity contest; you're there because you have a job to do.

Your assertiveness often lands you in the position of directing others, whether it's in a recognized way as a supervisor or a less formal way as an outspoken unofficial leader. When people don't live up to your expectations, your first response is to get more aggressive and lean on them harder. (You might try a different approach later, but only if leaning on them doesn't work.) Other people call this being pushy; you call it being effective.

You like to be in charge and would prefer there not be a great deal of collaboration with other workers. But you do admire and respect others who do jobs that involve an element of decisive action and command, such as pilots, firefighters, sheriff's deputies, and rescue workers.

You want other people—both workers and customers—to respect you and acknowledge you as a leader. You enjoy answering questions and resolving complaints; you have confidence that others should and will see that you've done the job right. You also like interviewing and hiring workers. Most of all, of course, you enjoy leading people to accomplish a mission.

The Miscast RE

RE's want action, and not only do they want to be at the center of it, they want to be directing it. For an RE to feel the fullest sense of purpose there must be a mission with clear objectives and a measurable outcome. RE's don't do particularly well with ambiguity.

Jobs that require a lot of patience, a lot of collaboration, or a lot of seemingly thankless work—think social worker, teacher, or administrative assistant—are not a good fit. An RE in these kinds of jobs is likely to feel that work is pointless, and the lack of observable outcomes will probably be supremely frustrating. Having to get every decision rubberstamped by a supervisor will drive an RE crazy. In order to truly use their talents in ways that will make them feel good, RE's need to be able to see clear results and feel a sense of accomplishment when the results are achieved. They also need some degree of latitude to make their own decisions.

Picture Yourself as a Construction Foreman

You may spend some of your time in an office, but it's not much of your time, and it's not much of an office. It's probably the kind of place where you check in periodically but don't spend a lot of time sitting at a desk. You're more likely to be found working out of a trailer at a construction site or out and about in a truck, handling problems and pitching in.

You're in charge of guiding a job to completion—getting subcontractors in place, making sure they show up, finding materials, monitoring progress, deciding about hundreds of details, dealing with permits and inspectors. If the people you have in place aren't getting it done, you'll find somebody who will. You're the go-to person on the site; everybody knows that decisions go through you. Your cell phone rings a lot; and when it does, you don't spend a lot of time chatting. You get the problem solved and then go on with your day.

You know not only how to supervise your crew but also how to do most of their jobs. Building things is second nature to you, and you love to see a project evolve throughout a day or a week. To you, there's nothing so satisfying as looking at a house or a school that you built and knowing there was only an empty field just a few months ago.

As an RE, you lead by example. Often this means being the best at what you do. You may have risen to the top because of your expertise and your ability to take charge. However, you're not just a leader; you also like hands-on work, especially with equipment.

You lead by aggression, strength, or force of will. You're the captain of the ship, and anyone who doesn't follow your orders gets thrown overboard. You're in charge of a mission, one that must be accomplished—often by a deadline. Your people *will* get it done, because you'll make it happen. This is the kind of attitude that also makes RE's excellent firefighters, sheriffs, or pilots.

RE Education Requirements

For some RE's, specific education isn't necessary. On-the-job training is usually sufficient. Furthermore, RE's tend to naturally work themselves into leadership roles rather quickly. However, a few RE jobs usually do require bachelor's degrees: airline pilot, public safety manager (especially in larger metro areas), park and game superintendent, and (in some cases) construction manager. In addition, some RE jobs require managerial training, technical training in a specific trade, or a two-year associate's degree. Many RE's train in both management and a trade; this provides them with a pathway for promotion near the beginning of their careers.

RE Job Opportunities

When a job requires an aggressive, take-charge person chosen from among the ranks, an RE is the perfect fit. RE's thus have lots of job options, broadly spread across many industries. Furthermore, some RE's design their own jobs in order to put themselves in positions of authority. Even if RE's do start at the bottom, it does not take long for them to climb the ladder.

RE's have job options in both rural and metropolitan labor markets. They can easily run the sale barn in a small town or manage an industrial plant in a major city.

RE Celebrity

Amelia Earhart, pilot and aviator

Amelia Earhart was an RE. She was competitive, adventurous, and determined. Earhart was a noted American aviation pioneer and was the first woman to fly solo across the Atlantic Ocean. She set many other records, wrote best-selling books about her flying experiences, and supported the Equal Rights Amendment. She was instrumental in the formation of The Ninety-Nines, an organization for female pilots.

> *I want to do it because I want to do it.*
>
> —Amelia Earhart

RC Realistic/Conventional: The Technician
The RC credo: *Take the time to do it right.*

If you're Realistic/Conventional (RC), you're probably...

- *precise.* When someone asks you for the time, you'll say, "2:15 and about 40 seconds."
- *careful.* You pack your tools in a carton marked "fragile."
- *hands-on.* Your fingerprints are everywhere—except when you use your wet wipes to remove them.
- *into routine.* You like shaking up your cocktail, *not* your schedule.
- *task oriented.* Nobody will ever accuse you of shirking.
- *efficient.* You never take a leisurely approach to getting something done.
- *reserved.* You don't like to be the center of attention.
- *persistent.* You'll hang in there and figure out a way to get the results you need.

- *intense.* You can concentrate on your work for long periods of time without a break.
- *mechanically minded.* You like to follow the schematic, and you have the patience to do it.

The RC Brain

Remember at the start of this chapter, when we said Rs are the people who make things work? Well, the RC Code-Combo is the one that best embodies this description.

An RC has a natural gift for mechanical thinking. The RC brain is tuned in to how things are supposed to work and the ability to make it happen. That's why RC's make good service technicians, skilled tradespeople, production workers, builders, and installers.

If you're an RC, you were probably the kind of kid who liked to put together model cars or rockets or take apart and reassemble your bike. As an adult, you may be drawn to magazines like *Popular Mechanics*, and you're totally in your element at a hardware store. In fact, you may go there for no other reason than to look around and figure out what you should add to your toolbox. Regardless of what you do to pay the bills, you probably consider it your secondary job to fix things around the house, and it irks you to have to pay a specialist to come and do a job when you could have done it yourself.

In general, you're precise, and you rarely make mistakes because you're systematic and diligent. You can readily master jobs that require intense focus and precision.

You feel best when you know exactly what you are doing and what is expected of you. Repetitive tasks don't bother you, and you have the focus and persistence to finish a task others would find tedious. The neighbors may have looked puzzled when you dug up the concrete walk leading up to your house and showed up with a load of multicolored bricks. But a few days later they were amazed when they saw the perfectly laid, intricately crafted path you built.

In work and in your spare time, you'd prefer to focus on an area of specialization, and using your expertise gives you a great sense of accomplishment. You feel a lot of pride when a project is completed to your satisfaction.

Perhaps when you were younger, you became interested in a technical hobby, such as flying radio-controlled planes, souping up motorcycles, or tinkering with sewing machines. Today those kinds of tasks still get your motor running, even if you don't get to do them very often. You prefer your work, and your work hours, to be very structured. You like clear processes, patterns, routine, and schedules. You enjoy and excel at reading maps, diagrams, and instructional manuals.

How RC's Relate to Others

You don't spend a lot of time conversing about unnecessary topics, especially with your coworkers. Your discussions are usually short and to the point. In fact, you don't want any conversation while you're working, because you want to be able to focus.

You prefer a lot of your work to be done independently; unlike some other CodeCombos, you don't need to be constantly chatting with somebody in order to feel happy. It makes you feel good when your expertise can help somebody out, but honestly, pleasing people is not your primary motivation. You are happiest when you meet your own standards and accomplish the goals you set for yourself, not when you worry about what others think.

Speaking of standards, yours are very high, and you're liable to get agitated when you have to be around people who don't meet them. Because you prefer routine and familiarity, you are the kind of person who will remain loyal to an organization (or a partner) for many years as long as you feel treated with respect.

The Miscast RC

An RC needs a certain degree of independence and, like most R's, can become frustrated or bored when deprived of the chance to do something physical and tangible. An RC wants to be fixing computers, not staring at them all day, or installing light fixtures instead of selling them.

That said, an RC can find a certain degree of contentment in a job that isn't a perfect match by finding a niche as a handyperson or go-to person when problems arise. Some RC's may also find themselves helping people in their spare time; for instance, an RC who works as a mail carrier may wind up talking to an elderly person on his route and coming back after work hours to help fix the dishwasher.

Overall, though, an RC who works in a job that simply pays the bills will probably always feel less happy at work than at home in the workshop.

Paul's Story

Paul had worked for Machinery Inc. as a hands-on mechanical technician for ten years. He built prototypes and worked on the floor. Because of his expertise and excellent problem-solving skills, Paul became a favorite of the mechanical engineers since he did his job so well. He could build anything. Paul's codes were RC, Realistic and Conventional, a perfect match for the mechanical technician job he enjoyed very much.

Because of the quality of his work, the engineers wanted to promote Paul to an engineering technician job. The codes for this job, RI, Realistic and Investigative, were different from his RC job. Paul did not want the promotion because it required more theory and math than the hands-on position he was doing. He declined the offer to change jobs several times. Every time he thought about the engineering technician job, he felt stressed. But the engineers were persistent, and he finally took the job against his better judgment.

Paul felt like a fish out of water. He did not feel capable of doing all the technical parts of the job. Within six months of taking it, he had a heart attack. Paul believed this was caused by the stress of his employment because he was not well matched to his work environment or job duties. He wished he had never left his mechanical technician job.

Picture Yourself as a Service Technician

Your skills are specialized and highly useful, and that means you're in demand.

Maybe you spend your days driving around town to fix things—power lines, or furnaces, or copy machines—or install them. Or maybe you are on call to handle problems within a building or a complex of buildings. People are usually happy to see you, because you take a load off their minds; when you arrive, that means a problem is going to get fixed.

You may work out of your truck, and if so, it probably accommodates all your tools, which are organized carefully in boxes and compartments for easy access. The truck is tidy, organized, and well equipped.

You enjoy paying attention to the details to help solve a problem, and you like to use your hands for precision tasks. You don't waste time; in fact, because you know what you're doing, you're usually fast and efficient. However, you do take the time to do things right.

You like to operate machinery and are careful in inspecting the necessary parts, making assessments, and setting calibrations.

You like to argue with other technicians about how something should be installed, fixed, or maintained, because you know your way is the best. You feel fulfilled when you have identified the problem and applied the correct solution.

Other ideal jobs for RC's might be found at a factory, a construction site, a metalworking shop, a medical office, or a lab. RC's also often work with very specialized and technical machines, such as those used in sound recording, lighting, or medical and dental fields. Anywhere you find the need for specialized expertise—which is almost everywhere—you might find an RC.

RC Education Requirements

Some RC jobs require formal technical training, from six-month certification programs to two-year associate's degrees. However, it is not uncommon for RC's to train on the job—either formally, as interns or apprentices, or informally.

RC Job Opportunities

More jobs are available to RC's than to people with any other CodeCombo. In fact, because RC's are suited to so many jobs, they sometimes have trouble choosing a specialization. RC's work in many industries, so in order to narrow down their career selection, they should first focus on an industry that they would most like to work in, and then select a specific job. RC's are needed in all labor markets, both rural and urban.

RC Celebrity

Jack Nicklaus, professional golfer and golf course designer
    Jack Nicklaus is an RC. He is athletic, skillful, and discriminating. Nicklaus is regarded by many as the greatest professional golfer of all time, with the most victories in major championships (eighteen). He now devotes much of

his time to golf course design and operates one of the largest golf design practices in the world.

> *My ability to concentrate and work toward that goal has been my greatest asset.*
>
> —Jack Nicklaus

———————

Connect with other "R's" & resources online at
www.CareerCode.com/R

CHAPTER 5

Investigative (I): The Thinkers

Nothing transforms our communities and the world faster than new ideas. It's been happening as long as people have been around—from the first time humans harnessed the power of fire, to the days when they figured out how to grow crops, to the medical breakthroughs that uncovered the role of bacteria in illness, all the way to current research in alternative energy that could again transform how the world operates.

At the forefront of these and countless other discoveries and advances, big and small, have been the thinkers—the scientists, researchers, scholars, doctors, theorists, and explorers. They are the people who have the brainpower and the drive to expand our knowledge about the universe and find bold new ways to solve the complex problems of the day. And most of these people are I's.

People whose dominant Interest Code is Investigative are the curious-minded ones who want to know everything about everything. They eat up information and are always hungry for more. They never want to stop learning, whether they are in school or not. The quest for knowledge excites them, and they have a genuine desire to understand, not just memorize facts. They are the kind of people who are not easily swayed, because they form their opinions and ideas based on observable and testable facts or on loads of research.

Because they often live in their heads and have confidence about their intellect, I's can at times seem introverted, hard to relate to, and maybe even egotistical. That's not on purpose—it's just the natural result of having an ever-growing and ever-complex internal dialogue and passion for information. For many I's, relating to others usually isn't as important as relating to knowledge.

If your first code is I, then you are very likely...

- logical
- scientific
- intellectual
- independent
- curious
- reserved

The I Interest Code

I's thrive on challenges, and they deliberate carefully about how to go about solving problems.

I's are very independent and need plenty of time alone so they can read, think, or reflect. An I would feel most at home reading scientific journals, analyzing data, conducting research, and exploring ideas. Not everyone who has strong I tendencies gets a chance to do those things for a living, but if you're an I, they are the kind of things that sound appealing. When the doctor says your child might have a developmental condition, do you go right home and find ten web resources and three books to help explain it? That's a classic I behavior. When somebody raises an interesting political or philosophical question over dinner, do you spend a few days thinking about it, only to bring it up again after everybody else has forgotten about it?

When I's are interested in a topic, they become fixated on understanding it completely. I's don't just read a book; they delve deeply and find other sources to investigate.

I's like to be respected for their intelligence, and they tend to prefer careers with a great deal of status, often becoming professors, doctors, economists, and psychologists. These careers require long and intensive education, but that is no problem for I's. By nature, I's are lifelong students.

How I's Can Get in Trouble

I's require a great deal of intellectual stimulation. If you don't fly at their level, they are not interested in spending much time with you. This can make I's seem condescending or aloof.

I's like to work alone and may be unapproachable when they are deep in thought. They do not like interruptions, which break their concentration. I's often escape the real world through their work. They do not watch the clock when they are involved in a project.

I's obsess about their attempts to learn, and they love to show off what they know. Sometimes they unintentionally chase others away by discussing a subject too deeply or going off on a tangent others find confusing.

They can sometimes get aggressive and attack—but with their intellects instead of their muscles. They are judgmental and will sometimes pick arguments with people who have different opinions. Some I's may be unpopular at work. They are often standoffish and would rather be right than be friends.

Education for I's

I jobs usually require a bachelor's degree at least, and most demand a graduate degree as well. I's are by far the most educated of the six CareerCodes, in part because they love to learn. In fact, sometimes I's delay selecting a college major because they are interested in so many different subjects.

I CodeCombos

- IR: The Scientist
- IA: The Scholar
- IS: The Practitioner
- IE: The Innovator
- IC: The Examiner

ⅠⓇ Investigative/Realistic: The Scientist

The IR credo: *The important thing is to never stop questioning.*
—*Albert Einstein*

If you're Investigative/Realistic (IR), you're probably...

- *scientific.* You read *Scientific American* for fun.
- *logical.* You rely on facts, not emotions, to arrive at conclusions.
- *analytical.* Breaking things down helps you figure out how to repeat successes—and avoid failures.
- *mathematical.* You're the one who always gets to figure out the probability of something happening.
- *highly intelligent.* Your brain is almost always tuned to its highest setting.
- *an avid reader.* That's one reason why you know so much.
- *very curious.* While others are reading celebrity gossip columns, you're reading about the newest discoveries of quantum physics.
- *egocentric.* You know how smart you are, and you're not about to apologize for it.
- *inquisitive.* Looking for answers is your idea of a treasure hunt.
- *critical.* To you, finding fault solves problems.

The IR Brain

If you're an IR, there is no search more important to you than the quest for answers, and you are willing to work your whole life in pursuit of them. It's not enough just to accumulate knowledge. If you work in an IR field, you may have had to memorize periodic tables or anatomical terms in college, but the real thrill comes from applying that knowledge to test a hypothesis, find a new solution to a problem, help a patient, or uncover new ways of understanding the world.

Even as a kid, an IR is easy to spot: She's the one who actually reads the informational placards at each of the zoo exhibits. Or he's the one who won the science fair—without any help from Dad—by coming up with a real, fascinating experiment while half the other kids took an easy route and grew some crystals in a jar. In high school, she was the one who worked summers at the state park, counting exotic plants in the wilderness.

For an IR, work is an extension of the need to explore and find answers, and the work must be challenging. When something is too easy, an IR has a hard time being attentive.

If you're an IR, you probably don't need a lot of incentive to get your work done. The work in itself is the reward. In fact, you don't want a supervisor breathing down your neck—you need autonomy to think things through. Once you're left alone, you'll get something done, even if you have to stay up all night. In fact, you'll often work long hours if you're feeling the flow.

You love to explore the unknown. You enjoy finding new solutions and reaching new, higher goals. You are motivated by challenges, especially those requiring unconventional thinking. If someone insists something is impossible, you will find a way to make it possible and find a way to logically defend it.

Maybe you get an opportunity to do this kind of exploration at work, but maybe you don't—and if that's the case, it's a problem for you. You will try to channel your curiosity and desire to explore into some other pursuit. Perhaps it gives you satisfaction to experiment with little things around the house, even something as small as trying five brands of laundry detergent and keeping track of which one does the best job for the money. Or maybe your passion for knowledge leads you to devour nonfiction books or subscribe to *Smithsonian*, *Discover*, and *Popular Mechanics* magazines to read in your spare time. Sitting on the porch by yourself—reading, thinking, processing—is your way of recharging your batteries.

How IR's Relate to Others

As a general rule, you want others to respect your intellect, and you're in heaven when others are impressed. You like to be around interesting people who have something to say that you haven't heard before, but small talk bores you to tears. You'd rather avoid company-sponsored social events; in fact, most of the time you dislike large gatherings, unless it's a room filled with other intellectually stimulating people.

When it comes to getting things done, you don't have the patience to manage or babysit other workers. You like to set up an experiment but prefer to avoid the day-to-day management of the study. Instead, you'll try to find someone competent—and someone who gets it the first time you explain the process—to handle it.

You are highly competitive with your peers and colleagues—especially those you consider to be your intellectual equals (though these are few and far between). You like to feel that your hard work and research has paid off and made you smarter than others, and when you feel threatened, you are motivated to work harder to get ahead.

The Miscast IR

An IR needs work that stimulates the mind, or things aren't likely to go well. It's very hard for an IR to check his or her brain at the door and just do a job for the paycheck alone.

In a job that does not allow for enough autonomy, an IR is the kind of employee who will drive a supervisor nuts, and there might be a lot of friction in such a situation. If you're an IR, you're likely to question why things are done the way they are, rather than simply follow orders, and if you don't agree with whomever's in charge, you're liable to do it your own way and let your boss deal with it. At the same time, being the boss holds no appeal for you, and middle management—the kind of job where you don't get a lot of say in big decisions but have to get other workers to fall in line—sounds like a recipe for permanent heartburn.

A classic IR wants a career that in some way contributes to the expansion of the human race's accumulated knowledge or at least applies that knowledge to solve problems. It's a grand aspiration, and not everybody is cut out for such a role. But it's what an IR needs in order to feel fulfilled, and in the absence of this opportunity, an IR may never be comfortable with his or her role in the world.

Picture Yourself as a Biologist

As a biologist, it's your mission to study and better understand the fundamental ways in which life works or apply that knowledge to a commercial field such as agriculture or medicine.

You spend a fair amount of time in a laboratory, where you perform research into unanswered questions. You might conduct experiments involving animals or plants— perhaps study how an octopus adapts to new environments or test the usefulness of a plant extract to treat disease. Depending on your specialty, you might get out into the field to examine organisms in their natural environment.

You get a lot of chances to do hands-on work, but you also spend time writing reports about your findings, perhaps even submitting your work to peer-reviewed journals. You may need to focus attention on convincing a university, a federal agency, or a private employer to fund your research.

You probably specialize in a field such as marine biology (the study of ocean life), botany (the study of plants), or microbiology (the study of bacteria and other microscopic organisms).

IR Education Requirements

Given the scientific focus of this CodeCombo, the educational path for many IR's is a graduate degree in a scientific field. However, for IR's who work in computing fields, a bachelor's degree is often sufficient. There are few jobs for IR's that do not require at least a four-year degree, and many demand much more, especially for specialized doctors in distinct fields of medicine.

IR Job Opportunities

IR's have many career opportunities. Some already-plentiful jobs for IRs will likely be even more plentiful in the future. Demand is predicted to be especially high in the environmental, health, and information technology fields. This gives most IR's lots of labor market mobility. Many IRs are able to make lateral career moves that lead to higher earnings.

IR Celebrity

Albert Einstein, physicist and mathematician

Albert Einstein was an IR. He was academic, empirical, and inventive. Einstein was regarded as one of the most influential and best known scientists and intellectuals of all time. He is often known as the father of modern physics. In 1921, he received the Nobel Prize in physics for his services to theoretical physics and especially for his discovery of photoelectric effect. He developed the well-known Theory of Special Relativity, $E = MC^2$.

An equation is something for eternity.
—Albert Einstein

IA Investigative/Artistic: The Scholar

The IA credo: *Education is a progressive discovery of our own ignorance.* —*Will Durant*

If you're Investigative/Artistic (IA), you're probably...

- *highly observant.* You've analyzed your entire neighborhood just by watching and listening.
- *a deep thinker.* You're able to understand people in a detailed and complex way, and you're good at reading between the lines.
- *intuitive.* You can sense what's really behind a smile.
- *insightful.* People often ask you for advice, for good reason.
- *complex.* You are a human Rubik's Cube.
- *a researcher.* You're deeply intrigued by human behavior and always want to know more about it.
- *introverted.* Given the choice, you'll stay home to read rather than go to a party.
- *intellectual.* You routinely use your brain to study, analyze, and come to conclusions about the world, especially about your fellow human beings.
- *independent.* You figure things out on your own and don't need others to agree.
- *opinionated.* You study things so deeply that you're often sure you're right. As a result, you often challenge others' opinions.

The IA Brain

An IA, like the other Investigative CodeCombos, is driven by the desire to learn and, of course, investigate. The thing that distinguishes IA's, though, is the subjects in which they are interested. Most I's—IR's, especially—deal in tangible, measurable subjects and outcomes. But the Artistic tint of the IA combo is a little different. It draws IA's into a different kind of investigation. It's more an investigation of ideas, of connections between things, and of history and culture. It's much harder to pin down an IA than the other I Code-Combos, and as you'll find out later, it's far from the most marketable CodeCombo.

If you're an IA, you are an original thinker and a close observer. When you set out to perform a task, you know exactly what you want to do—and not do. You also know exactly what information or answer you are looking for, and you'll expend an immense amount of time and energy to find it.

You have the intellectual curiosity that is the hallmark of the Investigative CodeCombos, but you are more interested in the soft sciences than the hard ones—the sciences that explain how people act and why, such as sociology, psychology, anthropology, and history.

How IA's Relate to Others

If you're an IA, you believe you understand how the world works. You can be extremely critical because you see people and situations as they really are and don't have much patience with those who don't get it. You also have a difficult time trusting others, for the same reason.

Part of you thrives on being contrary. This can be an asset when a critical mind is needed—face it, having somebody around to point out flaws makes any effort stronger—though it won't necessarily win you many friends.

Because you are so complex, you never feel completely understood by more than a few people. You are not interested in small talk at work and would rather spend time debating and discussing intellectual concepts with your peers. Maybe you have to find stimulating conversations on the Internet because they're not exactly abundant in your daily life.

The Miscast IA

While some people, particularly those with strong R or C tendencies, would see the scholarly pursuits of an IA as tedious and even frivolous, the IA feels the same way about physical work, repetitive work, or any work that doesn't stimulate the mind to think "deep thoughts" or seek new understanding.

Unfortunately, that means few jobs will truly fit the bill for an IA. There just aren't a lot of ways to get paid a living wage to explore the kinds of subjects that an IA will find fascinating. Working for a university, a museum, or a similar institution that promotes learning is probably your best bet, but those job opportunities are relatively rare in terms of the entire labor market.

This mean a lot of people with IA tendencies are left to fend for themselves, pursuing their interests in their spare time. Some of them suffer jobs they couldn't care less about in order to pay the bills. Maybe an IA will take a job in the accounts payable department at a large college because being an employee means she can take as many classes as she wants for free. It's likely that no matter what the employment situation, an IA will have a library card and use it often or order books online on a weekly basis.

Matt's Story

Matt couldn't wait for college. He had many interests, and he enjoyed studying and researching. He quickly figured out his biggest problem would be choosing a specialization. After a year and a half of general study courses, he opted to major in psychology with a minor in ethnic studies. He enjoyed all his classes, and when he graduated, he took a job in human services at a nonprofit organization in the same city he went to college. He continued in this position for ten years, until he was laid off.

When Matt came to see Tracy, he had realized that a decade after graduating from college, he was still no closer to understanding what he really wanted to do. After Tracy gave him the CareerCode test, his score revealed what she anticipated: Matt was an IA (Investigative and Artistic) with a third code of C (Conventional). Tracy showed Matt all the programs that IAs usually liked. Then she showed him how few jobs were available for IA's. She mentioned that many IA's find themselves in a similar situation to his. While Matt felt a bit relieved, he was hopeful that CareerCode could help him find a specialization.

CareerCode did exactly that. Since Matt's third code was C, technical writing was a good fit. Because he was naturally a strong writer, he did not need much additional training, and many technical writing jobs were available in his area.

Picture Yourself as a Sociologist

Your job is to research and gain an understanding of human systems that permeate a society's way of life—entire cultures as well as their smaller components, such as social groups and human institutions. You observe, collect data, and spend hours analyzing your findings in order to shed light on why people act the way they do in different circumstances. You are always putting together a puzzle, sifting through the interlocking pieces all around to find out how they fit together.

You may work for the government—in fact, according to the US Bureau of Labor Statistics, about 43 percent of social scientists do—and your findings could have a big influence on public policy. Maybe you study how racial and gender differences affect employees in the workplace, and your research could help shape legislation on employment law. Or perhaps you focus on how urban sprawl has affected people's driving habits over the past fifty years; your analysis could be important in urban planning and the development of mass transit.

Other sociologists are scholars who write books about past or present civilizations or important social issues. They may work for universities or nonprofit advocacy groups. As a sociologist, understanding others' research or doing original research to identify patterns of behavior is an integral part of your job. You can become completely lost in your research, spending long hours focused on finding the smallest detail that will help you understand interpersonal and cultural relationships. Libraries and research centers are some of your closest friends.

Because it's necessary for you to explain your efforts and conclusions to others, you have excellent writing and public speaking skills, and you use them as often as possible in your work. You may be a sought-after expert in your field, the kind who gets asked to be a guest on radio call-in shows.

You are typically surrounded by bookshelves filled with reference materials, as well as historical, artistic, and cultural artifacts. Being published in a venue with high professional prestige is the ultimate honor for you. So is speaking to a professional organization about your research and opinions.

IA Education Requirements

IA jobs require at least a bachelor's degree, and most IA careers require at least one graduate degree as well, plus specialized training, usually obtained through related work or additional focused study. Social scientists are among the professions whose members have the highest level of education. Strong analytical skills, including statistics and mathematical and quantitative research methods, are essential.

IA Job Opportunities

IA's often work in environments that support original research efforts, such as colleges and universities, libraries, historical societies, and museums.

IA's beware: there are very few job opportunities for you. Thus many IA's hold jobs that don't match their CodeCombo in order to make ends meet, while pursuing research projects or avocations on the side. Others use their creativity to design their own jobs and serve as consultants.

IA Celebrity

Sigmund Freud, neurologist and founder of psychoanalysis

Sigmund Freud was an IA. He was scholarly, experimental, and perceptive. Freud is best known for his theories of the unconscious mind. In academia, his ideas continue to influence the social sciences. His originality and intellectual influence made him one of the most prominent thinkers of the first half of the twentieth century.

> *The conscious mind may be compared to a fountain playing in the sun and falling back into the great subterranean pool of subconscious from which it rises.*
>
> —Sigmund Freud

IS Investigative/Social: The Practitioner

The IS credo: *Help others to heal—and do no harm.*

If you're Investigative/Social (IS), you're probably…

- *caring.* You are deeply concerned with the well-being of others.
- *diagnostic.* You revel in unraveling mysteries and diagnosing problems, whether it's why the oven isn't working, why your daughter has been acting somber, or how your buddy's golf swing is out of whack.

- *cautious.* You think it's best to move ahead carefully, so as not to cause harm.
- *curious.* You want to understand as well as help. Knowing what to do without knowing why makes you uneasy.
- *analytical.* You'll find meaning, information, connections, or patterns where most other people don't.
- *overextended.* Whether it's in family life, social circles, or the professional world, you take on more than you have time when you feel like a lot of people need your help.
- *independent.* You don't like to rely on anybody besides yourself or a few trusted confidants or staff members.
- *intellectual.* Perhaps you read scientific and trade journals in your spare time, or maybe you are drawn to books, news stories, or documentaries that get your mind working.
- *objective.* In any critical situation, whether it's a breakdown at work or a quarrel between your siblings, you know it's important to form unbiased, fact-based conclusions before making any judgments.
- *introverted.* You feel best when you're in a small group of others like you.

The IS Brain

Healthcare is an ideal career field for those with an IS CareerCode, because so much of the work revolves around helping others, thinking objectively, and solving challenging problems. An IS will feel deeply satisfied in a healthcare job that involves frequent contact with patients or staff, a job that's important and makes a difference for others. The IS is responsible and cool under pressure, and may thrive in an environment where emergencies can break out at any time.

If you're an IS, you set high standards for yourself. A doctor, for instance, realizes that his or her assessment of patients' physical or emotional conditions can have a dramatic effect on their lives. For the same reasons, an IS is typically methodical, analytical, precise, and cautious.

How IS's Relate to Others

Whether you work in a cubicle or a clinic, you are known for your ability to handle a large workload, although you sometimes get prickly when you have a lot to do. You realize you cannot do your job without the cooperation and collaboration of coworkers, but you may become short-tempered if you are overworked or overextended because you want enough time for face to face contact.

You recognize the value of other highly trained professionals, and you call on their expertise whenever necessary. You enjoy expanding your knowledge base because it makes you feel good to know that you're always developing as a professional. You're willing to help out your colleagues when they need it.

Accepting help is another story—it is difficult for you to delegate work tasks; you don't like to let go because you believe you are the best person to make the right decisions.

The Miscast IS

If your CareerCode is Investigative and Social, you may feel bored by tasks that require a lot of repetition. Doing the same thing over and over, especially if it involves data or paperwork as opposed to people, just doesn't stimulate you. You may find yourself getting distracted and spending a little too much time by the coffee maker, chatting with a coworker. You surf the Web, reading articles that make you think, or you lurk on discussion boards where people are sharing their problems and offering each other solutions.

Sometimes you feel your work doesn't make a difference. If you didn't show up, would anybody notice? If your work didn't get done, would it be that big of a deal? Even if you can convince yourself the work is important, you might find it lacking intellectually.

Maybe you try to get that sense of intellectual and interpersonal satisfaction in your spare time. You might do this in a hands-on capacity by volunteering to counsel troubled kids or help out with the blood drive at the community center. Maybe you do it vicariously by getting engrossed in fast-paced TV shows like *ER* or mysteries like *CSI*—or, better yet, science and health programming on the Discovery Channel. In your group of friends, you may be known as the one who's always helping the others figure out their problems and solve them. This gives you the kind of fulfillment you need.

Picture Yourself as a Health Practitioner

You work in a busy clinic or hospital, seeing patients all day long who need your help. Your mind is always going as you move from one to the next, deciphering symptoms and answering questions. But you don't feel overwhelmed; you feel invigorated.

Computer technology gives you instant access to test charts, results, and other important information. You analyze each case individually and pay diligent attention to every detail. You are committed to your job and your patients, and you will work long hours to serve them. Sometimes you're on call, and during these times, you could get a page or a phone call at any moment, calling you in to perform an emergency procedure or asking your advice on a tricky case.

Your schedule is tight, fast paced, and typically arranged by others. You have little control over the scheduling and never feel you have enough time to see everyone and do everything. You are interested in the social good, but that is secondary to your evaluation and diagnostic focus. In working with your patients, you are deliberate and cautious, performing tests that help rule things in or out. You typically spend most of your professional time in a hospital or clinic. You may work alone in an office reviewing charts and test results as well as with patients in examination rooms, hospital rooms, or specialized treatment areas.

You thrive on making the correct diagnosis, especially in exceptionally difficult cases. You get great satisfaction from seeing a recommended treatment work and from making a positive difference in people's lives.

IS Education Requirements

IS's who are MDs must of course complete both a bachelor's degree and medical school. Those in certain specialties must also complete additional professional training. You don't need to be a doctor to be happy as an IS; some IS's earn undergraduate or graduate degrees in other health professions or work in fields where they assist clients or students in other ways.

IS Job Opportunities

There is a great and ongoing need for IS's. Since most IS jobs are in healthcare, the special IS CareerCode, representing a scientific approach with a service orientation, will remain in high demand, especially as our population ages.

Jobs in certain medical and health specialties are far more plentiful in large metropolitan areas, while more general IS jobs (family practitioner, physician's assistant, chiropractor) are widely available everywhere.

IS Celebrity

Dr. Mehmet Oz, cardiac surgeon and host of *The Dr. Oz Show*

Dr. Oz is an IS. He is highly educated, informative, and patient oriented. Oz became a household name by making frequent appearances on *The Oprah Winfrey Show*. He obtained joint MD and MBA degrees from the University of Pennsylvania School of Medicine and the Wharton School of Business. His passion is bringing awareness about many different diseases and health-related problems to the public and educating the masses about preventative measures.

> *When you've finally climbed the last technology mountain and the patient still doesn't feel well, that's when we start looking in areas... like spirituality and alternative therapies that bridge cultures of healing.*
> —Dr. Mehmet Oz

IE Investigative/Enterprising: The Innovator
The IE credo: *We turn challenges into opportunities.*

If you're Investigative/Enterprising (IE), you're probably...

- *competent.* You are accomplished, and you get results.
- *a critical thinker.* You love to think and analyze. For you, it's fun.
- *curious.* You want to know exactly how everything functions.
- *an expert.* Your knowledge is highly technical and often unique.
- *persuasive.* You can talk people into almost anything when you set your mind to it.
- *a systems thinker.* You enjoy laying out the entire project—on paper, on your computer, or in your head.
- *opinionated.* (You would prefer to call it "confident and assured.")
- *strategic.* Every move you make is calculated.

- *entrepreneurial.* Your million-dollar ideas keep you awake at night.
- *competitive.* You play to win.
- *sharp.* You are astute and quick to understand how things work.

The IE Brain

All of the I CodeCombos tend to thrive as investigators, gatherers of knowledge, and keepers of specialized expertise. The Enterprising element of the IE combo adds a new element: the ability to size up abstract and complicated situations and apply knowledge to solve problems in ways that others may not have thought of. That's why we've labeled IEs "The Innovators."

If you're an IE, you enjoy investigating, researching, and evaluating a situation, and then presenting a solution—often very persuasively. When you worked in small groups during classes in high school or college, you were probably the one itching to make your group's presentation to the whole class. When you served on the local school district's building committee, you threw yourself into the task of evaluating the options for expanding the elementary school, maybe even pointing out possibilities nobody else had thought of, and once you found what you considered the best choice, you lobbied the others to go along with your plan.

Your best fit would be a job that is highly specialized, requiring a significant amount of insight, education, and skill, because you like to be involved in projects that require a great deal of study and analysis. You love challenges. You want to be the go-to person on all projects, and you want to be acknowledged as the leader. As a result, you may have trouble with project managers, and may take on (or promise) too much.

Because you're a careful researcher who possesses a strong intellect, you genuinely feel that you can do the most successful job on almost any task, so it seems natural to take the lead. This sincere desire to reach the best possible outcome motivates you to take charge.

But you are also motivated by recognition: you get a rush when others recognize your diligence and skill. Being published in a professional journal or being selected to teach a seminar to peers or allied professionals deeply satisfies you. You enjoy steadily building a résumé that reflects your accomplishments.

How IE's Relate to Others

You have strong opinions, and you're skilled at communicating them, which makes you a powerful presence in the room. You stop short of dominating socially or being a social butterfly, but you're ready with your opinions, and you're capable of wowing a crowd when you start talking about a topic that passionately concerns you.

In professional situations, you are equally at home working alone or with others. In fact, you need some of each. You thrive in an environment where you participate in strategic team meetings as well as do your own research. You need some degree of freedom to work alone and come to your own conclusions, but you also need to work closely with others in order to communicate your findings, collaborate, and pitch your ideas. You enjoy this process, but only if your colleagues are at your level.

Because you are independent and academically accomplished, you may not care to spend much time with subordinates, and you may not be patient or careful in explaining to others the tasks they need to complete. Often you make the mistake of thinking that your subordinates understand more than they do. You forget that very few fly at your level.

You may feel comfortable working with more than one team. You actually appreciate the stimulation of different projects and having your expertise sought out.

The Miscast IE

An IE fits best in a job that allows some latitude to work on a variety of projects, as well as opportunities to follow where ideas lead. Therefore, any job where employees are expected to follow strict protocol is definitely a bad match.

IE's are big-picture thinkers. Getting bogged down in the little details of making things work—things like scheduling appointments, answering the phone, and collating papers—only holds them back from reaching their objectives. Besides, it's boring. In fact, some entrepreneurs, many of whom have a strong IE bent, will start a company and nurture it for a while until it becomes business as usual, then sell and start a new company rather than stick around and handle the day-to-day operations of the old one.

Most IE's will languish in jobs where there's no concrete reward, other than a paycheck, to look forward to. IE's love the satisfaction of finishing a project and basking in its success, or the thrill of discovering something new and finding a way to market it to somebody else. The "daily grind" of doing the same thing over and over, with no end in sight, would probably depress an IE.

Picture Yourself as a Technical Consultant

As a consultant, you're a hired gun brought in to solve a problem or assess a situation that your client doesn't have the expertise or time to address. Your work life is varied; you could find yourself involved with different projects in different places from month to month. If you're an environmental consultant, for instance—one of the largest specialties within the technical consulting field—you might help create a cleanup plan for a contaminated urban site for one project and next find yourself working with a high-tech manufacturing company helping it develop a plan to meet tightened environmental regulations.

Your scientific knowledge and skills are highly valuable and in demand—and that means you're well respected and well compensated. But you can't get by on your knowledge alone—you also need to be an opportunistic and creative thinker who's quick to size up a situation and go straight for the right tool in your mental toolbox.

Your work tasks are typically scientific and involve measurement, calculation, and research. In order to describe the results of your analysis in terms the client can understand, you need to use your strong persuasive skills.

You spend half of your time consulting with others on projects and the other half devoted to thought and analysis. You strive to be current and informed about technological changes by reading scientific, technical, or business journals and other academic materials. You enjoy being challenged.

Your job might involve some selling—indeed, there's always an element of salesmanship in securing a client and getting repeat business—but you close the sale not through a hard sell but by consistently turning in high-quality work.

Because you manipulate data in order to better understand problems and potential solutions, you prefer to have a quiet work space with your computer, analytical tools, and reference materials nearby. You probably also have a similarly well-equipped home office.

IE Education Requirements

Almost all IE jobs require postsecondary education. In fact, the minimum IE educational path is the completion of a bachelor's degree—and often a graduate degree as well—in a specialized area of software, engineering, analysis, or management.

IE Job Opportunities

Job opportunities for IE's—especially those who specialize in engineering, computer technology, or market research and analysis—are very good. Because recruiters actively seek experienced IEs to fill a variety of specialized job openings, IE's can often relocate relatively easily. In some instances, IE's are hired for project work rather than as salaried employees.

IE Celebrity

Warren Buffett, businessman

Warren Buffett is an IE. He is a famous businessman, investor, and philanthropist who is analytical, insightful, and decisive. He is one of the most successful investors in the world and the primary shareholder and CEO of Berkshire Hathaway. Buffet is well-known for his devotion to the philosophy of value investing as well as for his personal frugality despite his immense wealth.

> *For some reason, people take their cues from price action rather than from values. What doesn't work is when you start doing things that you don't understand or because they worked last week for somebody else. The dumbest reason in the world to buy a stock is because it's going up.*
>
> —Warren Buffett

IC Investigative/Conventional: The Examiner

The IC credo: *An ounce of prevention is worth a pound of cure.*

If you're Investigative/Conventional (IC), you're probably...

- *a systematic thinker.* You're concerned with what is, not with what might be.
- *accurate.* You're careful and calculated—and, as a result, rarely wrong.

- *anal retentive.* Because you're so careful, methodical, deliberate, and accurate, you take it to
  the extreme.
- *cautious.* You observe, deliberate, decide, and
  plan before you act.
- *critical.* Part of being methodical is pointing out
  when other people aren't.
- *no fan of surprises.* No surprise birthday parties
  or spontaneous meetings for you.
- *deeply engaged with whatever you do.* You know
  how to focus, but the downside is that you can
  also get fixated. Others may even call you obsessive.
- *quick with calculations.* You can add up the credit
  card charges in your head faster than most people can pull out their cards.
- *opinionated.* Not about everything, but certainly
  about your area of expertise.
- *precise.* You'll work on something until it is absolutely perfect, correct, or ideal.
- *uncompromising.* You believe in doing things
  right—and know that your way is usually the
  right one.

The IC Brain

The IC is, first and foremost, methodical and careful. If
you're an IC, you investigate. You question things. You take
nothing at face value. And you can be relied on to compile
the information needed to answer a question.

If you're an IC, you play by the book. When you were a

kid, you were probably the one who opened the new board game and went immediately for the instructions, read every word of them, and strictly enforced the rules once you started playing. You've always loved to dig into big projects, from writing research papers in school to organizing closets to planning vacations, and you can find yourself getting lost in them, paying attention to every detail. You're reluctant to quit until everything is just right.

When it is time to a make decision on a big purchase, like a car, you dive into data about prices, resale value, fuel efficiency, reliability, warranties, and cargo space, and then crunch the numbers to get the most logical answer. (Maybe you even make a spreadsheet; that'd be a typical IC thing to do.)

You have excellent organizational skills and an exceptional ability to focus and "zone in." It is nearly impossible for you to work on more than one project at a time because you become consumed with whatever you're doing. You are bright and efficient, so most things in your life get done because you are organized, such as updating your spreadsheets, making the grocery list, and picking up the dry cleaning.

You're a perfectionist, but you're also aware that nothing is ever perfect. You are extremely moral and ethical, and you've always been strident about following proper procedures and rules. In your mind, these are not arbitrary but were created to ensure safety and accuracy.

You are hardworking and willing to put in long hours to do things right. In fact, it's probably hard to shut yourself off. Other folks may cut out early on a Friday afternoon or show up for a class without reading the assignment beforehand, but cutting corners that way doesn't interest you.

It feels good to know that what you do is valued and important, and this alone is enough to get you out of bed in the morning. You feel deeply responsible—and, truth be told, you enjoy having big responsibilities.

How ICs Relate to Others

You can be very critical of coworkers when they don't live up to your standards.

You probably do not enjoy a lot of (or even any) collaboration. You're willing to work on a team when necessary, but even then you need your autonomy. Having too many people around makes things too complicated. Plus, no one else can handle your specialty as well as you.

Because your work requires intense focus and precision, you're not one to socialize during—or maybe even after—work or school. You use so much energy on the important tasks of the day that by the time you're done, you just want to go home and recharge. You do like to use the computer even for relaxation.

The Miscast IC

As we said earlier, IC's are systematic thinkers who dive into clearly defined projects and see them through to completion. Lots of jobs, however, don't mix well with those tendencies, and that spells trouble for an IC.

Management is not a good fit, because dealing with people is not like dealing with data. People are much more unpredictable—and often maddening. Emotions and psychology come into play. Outcomes are not always known. People don't always follow the rules. Communication breaks down. It's pretty much an IC's nightmare.

There are lots of other situations where an IC will feel annoyed or overwhelmed: an IC will probably see most physical labor as pointless, and any situation where things are disorganized, hectic, or unpredictable will be hard to swallow. Being a doctor or a nurse who's running from patient to patient and getting paged during dinner doesn't hold much appeal.

ICs will tend to impose order on their environment in any way they can, so even if they're in a job that's a bad fit, they'll try to get satisfaction out of implementing new organizational techniques or ways of getting work done that will improve efficiency. (Then they'll probably throw up their hands in frustration when other people don't use them the right way.)

Picture Yourself as an Actuary

An IC is adept at gathering and compiling large amounts of data into structured formats so it can be further analyzed, studied, and examined. That fits the job description of an actuary to a T.

As an actuary, you work for the insurance or financial services industry, or maybe for the government. It's your job to go through reams of data and evaluate risk, and the information you compile is used to determine pricing and policies for insurance and financial products. For example, some actuaries help auto insurance companies determine how much they can expect to pay in claims, which helps them decide how much to charge their customers. To do this, actuaries use probability tables, modeling software, and other techniques to predict the financial cost of claims by drivers depending on their age, gender, location, driving history, type of car, and so forth.

Math and logic are your areas of strength, and you have a high degree of computer literacy. You also need good communication skills to explain your work to higher-ups in the company and, sometimes, to the public.

You're always looking for trends and patterns, and you assemble and package information to make it useful for decision making. You must tightly control your work, since so much is at stake and one small error can dramatically alter the results. Many people rely on your accuracy, and an error can make a major difference for customers or your organization.

Because part of your job is to find potential problems and flaws, you are always looking for inconsistencies and irregularities.

You're also patient; being an actuary means working for several years in a junior position while working your way up to higher levels of certification by passing a series of exams that test your knowledge about the industry and its methods.

IC Education Requirements

Because IC's typically work with research or statistics, most IC jobs require at least a bachelor's degree. The study required for IC jobs is usually difficult and requires intense concentration—just like actual IC jobs.

IC Job Opportunities

Although there are very few *types* of IC jobs, the total number of available IC jobs is large. The IC skill set is in high demand in many fields: business and finance, economics, insurance, laboratory research, pharmaceuticals, regulation, and technology. IC's who specialize in a particular field can often achieve high positions and make a lot of money.

IC Celebrity

Judy Sheindlin, host of syndicated TV show, *Judge Judy*

Judge Judy is an IC. She is inquisitive, discerning, and judicious. Sheindlin is a lawyer, judge, and author. New York Mayor Ed Koch appointed her as a judge in criminal court because he liked her no-nonsense attitude. She continued to be promoted and earned a reputation as a tough judge. After her retirement, she developed a syndicated courtroom television show, *Judge Judy*, featuring real cases with real rulings.

> *I don't care what you think! I'm the one who has to make a determination what is fair.*
>
> —Judge Judy

Connect with other "I's" & resources online at
www.CareerCode.com/I

CHAPTER 6

Artistic (A): The Creators

When talking about what it takes to do a job well, we often use words such as "skill" or "training" or "expertise." Those words imply something that is acquired or something that can be learned. As we've seen in the last two chapters, these characterizations are only partly true. Yes, skills and expertise can be learned, but there's also a strong element of innate ability that goes into what people are good at—and what they enjoy doing.

In no Interest Code is the idea of innate ability more dominant than in the A, or Artistic, code. When talking about artistic people, we tend to abandon terms like "training" and "know-how" and instead use the word "talent." Of all the Interest Codes, the A's are the ones most associated with that hard-to-define and easy-to-admire quality: talent. The A's are wellsprings of natural ability, and they are often seen as doing things that other people could simply never do, no matter how much training and practice they have.

Being artistic does take talent, but it also takes hard work and dedication. As we will see in exploring the Artistic CodeCombos, there are as many different ways to be creative and as many ways to apply that creativity to work as there are paintings in the Louvre. And while talent is one thing that most Artistic types have in common, the more important quality they share is their outlook on life and work. Most don't see creating things as a job. It's not just the means to an end. They are driven to create because it fills their soul. They create because they couldn't imagine *not* doing it. It's how they express themselves and how they relate to the world. Most A's have a deep need to do both of these things in order to feel happy.

A's are our actors, our entertainers, our dancers. They are painters, poets, and playwrights. You'd expect to see their work in a theater or a museum, but even in an inconspicuous place like the supermarket, their influence is everywhere: they wrote the novels and magazines that are for sale in the checkout lines, designed the apron of the employee who bags your groceries, composed the music that's playing over the store's sound system, and created the advertisement that brought you to the store in the first place.

If your first code is A, then you are very likely…

- idealistic
- imaginative
- expressive
- original
- creative
- independent

The A Interest Code

A's are imaginative, emotive, idealistic, and intense. They each have their own unique style and image. However, they all share the desire to create, and they often spend just as much time taking in the creative efforts of others because they need regular inspiration—from concerts, art exhibits, fashion, or movies. They can also find their muse through traveling or interacting socially.

In their work as well as their personal lives, A's don't have much use for moderation. It's usually all or nothing. Not surprisingly, most A's are risk takers by nature. (The Artistic/Conventional CodeCombo is the one exception.)

When A's are inspired, they can work for hours on adrenaline alone. But A's can also be easily bored, especially if their work doesn't provide enough change. This is when the A may choose to shake things up by rearranging the office furniture or painting the walls. A's need sensory stimulation at work, whether it is from colors, fabrics, stories, candles, music, or food.

Most A's need unstructured work environments so they can feel free to create. They don't work well in places where they feel boxed in; they need bigger, free-form spaces. And they need to feel they can get right to work when the inspiration strikes. They may spend hours languishing, trying to finish a piece, and then quit in frustration before suddenly feeling inspired and rushing to get back to their work.

A's can be their own worst critics because they expect their projects to be perfect.

How A's Can Get in Trouble

Because A's are naturally dramatic and expressive, they often emote without thinking. They may say exactly what's on their minds without regard for other people's feelings. Furthermore, because A's are idealistic, they can become very critical of themselves or others, and they may oscillate between optimism and disillusionment about what they do and how the world works.

A's don't usually mean to offend others; they just want whatever they are involved with to be better. However, sometimes they have a problem delivering this message nicely.

A's are usually theatrical, and it shows up in their work life and interactions. They may embellish when talking about coworkers, which can stir up trouble. They are drama queens.

A's can be brilliant, but sometimes they aren't dependable. They can miss deadlines, come to work late, blow off scheduled appointments, and fail to plan ahead. And when they do, they usually feel little or no remorse.

Education for A's

The educational patterns for A's aren't as clear as those for the other five Interest Codes. In part this is because the educational requirements for many A jobs vary dramatically. If you're an aspiring actor, for example, you might earn a bachelor of fine arts degree in drama, and perhaps even a master of fine arts. Many well-known actors have BFAs and MFAs. But many other successful actors have no such formal training; instead, they just auditioned and appeared on stage as often as possible, typically in community theater and dinner theater before getting their big break. Still others may have taken a few improvisation and acting classes.

Because A's are creative people who tend to challenge preconceived notions and think outside the box, they can be entrepreneurs by nature. Some literally invent their own jobs or even entire new fields. But there's no guarantee their efforts will work on the first try. Many A's tell stories of failing dozens of times before their ideas catch on.

In general, it's hard to draw any kind of a box—educational or otherwise—around most A's because they value creativity and originality above everything.

The one notable exception is the Artistic/Conventional CodeCombo. Some very specific AC educational programs do exist. Most of these are in library science, arts administration, and museum studies. Many AC jobs require at least a bachelor's degree, and some require a master's degree in one of these specialized fields.

Most colleges and universities offer programs in the arts, including visual arts, writing, music, drama, dance, film, video, publication design, commercial art, and multimedia performance. Yet it's important to understand that comparatively few jobs and careers exist for A's. And although the talent factor we discussed earlier doesn't determine everything, it does play a big role in influencing who succeeds and who fails. Earning a BFA in dance doesn't mean you can easily land a job as a dancer with a dance company. That may take several more years of practice and unpaid performing, if it happens at all.

A CodeCombos

- AR: The Designer
- AI: The Idealist
- AS: The Artistic Nurturer
- AE: The Performer
- AC: The Critic

AR Artistic/Realistic: The Designer

The AR credo: *If I can see it, I can create it.*

If you're Artistic/Realistic (AR), you're probably...

- *visionary.* You see things as they should be, rather than how they are.
- *sensitive.* Criticism, even when it's constructive, stings.
- *inventive.* You have been known to create even in your sleep.
- *argumentative.* You challenge anyone who refuses to think outside the box.
- *meticulous.* You have an eye for detail.
- *patient with the artistic process.* You can create for hours without a break.
- *an architecture lover.* You get goose bumps touring a historic building.
- *into photography.* This means real photography—*not* snapshots taken with a disposable piece of

junk. You need quality equipment to produce quality results.

- *introverted.* Although people may fawn over your talent, you don't enjoy kibitzing with strangers, even if they admire you.
- *original.* Nothing about you is vanilla. Your clothing and your home are reflections of your artistic imagination.
- *internally focused.* You are often thinking about your place in the world.

The AR Brain

If you ask most people what an artistic person is like, they'll probably give a description that fits many AR's: Brilliant but sometimes quiet; perhaps moody and unpredictable; prone to spend hours meticulously painting, or developing photographs, or sculpting. The kind of person who spends time in art galleries—not only to look at the works of art, but to host a reception when his or her own work is on the walls. A perfectionist. An idealist.

If you're an AR, you have artistic vision combined with a hands-on ability to design and create things. You have what some would call a natural eye for beauty and design, and you're a spatial thinker who seems to have a sixth sense about how to make things look good. You may channel this into art, or if your artistic tendencies haven't bloomed (or have been repressed), this quality may express itself in your wardrobe, the way you keep your house, or even the way you arrange and adorn your workspace.

AR's often feel best when they express themselves through tangible art, not words. As a kid, did you find it easier to express your feelings if you drew a picture rather than if you talked about it? That's an example of what we're talking about.

You thrive on autonomy and independence. Conversely, you bristle at the idea of somebody watching over you. You're the best judge of when your work is done, and you can be your own worst critic. It is difficult for you to close the book on a project because there is always some way to make it better, even though others may consider it finished.

Some AR's can't easily find a job that lets them use their creative muscles. Even in a job that's a poor fit, an AR may search for the chance to do something tactile, visual, and creative. A nine-to-five office job may be dreary much of the time, but an AR will probably be first in line to volunteer when the boss needs somebody to make a company photo album or pick out new furniture for the waiting room.

AR's find themselves drawn to creative pursuits in their spare time, and they probably have some paints or a pottery wheel or a sewing machine tucked away somewhere that they'd like to spend more time with.

If you're an AR, you blossom when you get to show off your creativity, especially when it is appreciated and praised. You have deep respect for the study of art and architecture. Others may have slept through a college discussion of the art of the Italian Renaissance, but you hung on every word.

How AR's Relate to Others

You are confident about your ability and your field of expression, and you can be opinionated and critical about the work of others. But if people criticize your ideas, their words can cut deep.

Social climbing and hobnobbing with the rich and famous are not for you—unless they're interested in your creative work. Sometimes they are, and you're invited to their parties. Because you like to express yourself, it chafes when you have to go through the motions of social pleasantries. You'd rather keep it real in your relationships.

You may have a hard time collaborating in your work. Once you have a vision for how something should be, it's hard for you to see another person's viewpoint. You are confident of your own abilities and can be opinionated and critical about the work of others, including your coworkers, who may be executing your runway project. You can be irritable at times and may snap at coworkers without thinking, especially if your project is near a deadline.

The Miscast AR

Artistic talent is perhaps the most common quality that people with "real jobs" channel into hobbies in their spare time. Indeed, as we've seen, the AR's drive to create and work with something tactile and visual makes it very likely that they will find some kind of artistic outlet if the need isn't being fulfilled at work. But there may not be enough time to let their ingenuity fully bloom.

Creating something gives an AR a sense of purpose. Because AR's are often introspective, sensitive, and deep, they may often wonder about their place in the universe. They may find themselves bordering on an existential crisis if they don't feel like they are interacting with the world (and the world of ideas) by exploring an artistic medium.

Unfortunately, a passion for art is an area of interest that many people misunderstand. It's easily labeled by cynics as unrealistic or foolish when it comes to selecting a career. Well-meaning parents and guidance counselors may do everything in their power to talk an artistically inclined person out of pursuing a creative dream. Even practical fields such as fashion design or photography are low-paying at the entry level, and such fields can seem unpredictable and unstable. That means a lot of AR's feel pushed into professions that don't suit them. Before they know it, they're ten years into a career and feeling they've missed their true calling. But it's never too late; a miscast AR can find ways to rekindle an artistic interest and even change careers to pursue that elusive dream of being paid to create.

Picture Yourself as a Graphic Artist

Very few AR's are talented enough to be superstar artists. Just like most high school baseball players don't make the big leagues, most AR's don't make a fortune selling their original artwork. That doesn't mean an AR has to be a starving artist. Luckily, there are a variety of jobs where artistic vision and creativity intersect with commerce, and graphic design is one of them.

As a graphic artist, you may work for a large advertising or design firm that creates logos, signs, or ads for big clients. Or you may work as a freelance designer, possibly out of your home, picking up projects big and small and having more of a one-on-one relationship with customers. Your work might appear primarily on paper, but it may also wind up on the Web or even on film.

Your job is to convey a message through a design. Your artistic skills help make your designs eye-catching, distinctive, and visually pleasing, and your natural ability to manage space helps you arrange the elements in the optimal way. You're given latitude to explore ideas and to draw on your deep well of creativity.

You enjoy being given a challenge and then applying your creativity to the search for an answer. When you feel inspired, you get rolling and usually stay on a roll until you've finished. You love pitching your ideas to clients or supervisors, and you like it even more when your ideas are appreciated.

Sometimes your product fits the bill perfectly, and in those cases you feel great. At other times, you may have to compromise your vision to fit somebody else's desires, and this may frustrate you.

You need your own space, both literally and figuratively, and if you're a freelance designer, that may be your own studio. You need to be left alone to channel your ideas, and you need enough physical space to fulfill your artistic vision. If you use a computer, it is undoubtedly a Mac, for the PC is far too conventional for you, and Macs are better suited for the kinds of visual software that you require.

AR Education Requirements

Most AR jobs require a combination of innate talent and some college or specialty training. Many AR career paths require a two-year or four-year degree, from either an art and design school or a general college or university. A few AR jobs (such as Web designer, interior designer, or fashion designer) require specialized training or apprenticeships. An AR without training will struggle to find a suitable job.

AR Job Opportunities

Although there are many different AR career paths, the number of AR job openings is small. In general, AR jobs can be tough to find and get. Furthermore, most ARs have a particular ability or interest that takes them in a specific direction. An AR who can do well in fashion design is not likely to be just as interested in Web design or architecture.

Many AR's need to be strategic about where they search for jobs. Most AR jobs are in large metropolitan areas, particularly on both coasts. For example, Southern California is the center for film and television jobs; New York City is the center for jobs in fashion.

AR Celebrity

Nate Berkus, interior designer

Nate Berkus is an AR. He is imaginative, stylish, and natural. Berkus is an interior decorator. His Chicago firm is Nate Berkus Associates, and he was a regular guest on *The Oprah Winfrey Show*, offering decorating and design advice to viewers. Nate is the author of *Home Rules: Transform the Place You Live Into a Place You'll Love*, a step-by-step guide to home design and decoration. In 2010 he launched his own syndicated television show, *The Nate Berkus Show*.

> *I made my parents crazy. As a kid, I redecorated my bedroom every month.*
>
> —Nate Berkus

AI   Artistic/Investigative: The Idealist

The AI credo: *An unexamined life is not worth living.*—Socrates

---

If you're Artistic/Investigative (AI), you're probably…

- *intensely verbal.* Words are your paintbrush.
- *expressive.* You are only truly happy when you are creating.
- *private.* When you want to reveal your thoughts, you write.
- *opinionated.* You have strong feelings, and you're very willing to express them in detail, using an impressive vocabulary.
- *well-read.* Learning and exercising your brain are essential to your mental health.
- *somewhat antisocial.* You prefer to interact with others in small doses.
- *highly idealistic.* The world would be so much better if it were exactly as you imagine it could be.
- *perpetually thinking.* You can't turn off your brain, even if you want to (which you don't).

- *intolerant.* Mundane people bore you to death, especially when their opinions and ideas are unsubstantiated.
- *extremely perceptive.* You can often sense the real meaning behind others' words and actions.

The AI Brain

The artistic focus of the A Interest Code, combined with the inquisitive nature of the I Interest Code, makes the AI well suited for creative writing and research. AI's are typically well-rounded thinkers who are interested in a wide range of academic subjects. They often have a unique perspective and are brimming with ideas, and they're good at using words to convey their ideas. They use language to explain, persuade, entertain, and enlighten.

If you are an AI, you are a soulful and deep thinker. You are also passionate. AIs need intellectual challenge and creative stimulation, or their minds tend to wander. An AI is the kind of person who can walk into a bookstore and not know where to begin, because every subject seems so interesting. If you're an AI, you need complete autonomy in order to think and create; once you get hold of a project that turns your crank, you can get so involved that you become a hermit until it's completed.

Does this sound like you? Whenever you move, you realize that the heaviest and most plentiful boxes are the ones containing your books. When it was time to write essays for college applications, you didn't dread the experience the way many of your peers did—rather, you already had five good ideas, and you looked forward to trying them out.

You'd rather write a paper on a book than take a test about it. You're idealistic and have strong opinions, which means you might feel pulled to be involved in politics—probably not by going out and shaking hands, but by writing letters to editors or senators or writing a blog with a political focus.

Sometimes you make a project more complex than it really needs to be, and you need help to focus. Similarly, while your creativity allows you to see multiple approaches to a project, that can mean you have trouble deciding which way to go.

You have high standards and ideals—some would even call you a perfectionist. You hold yourself and others to the same set of expectations. If everything isn't just right, you can get frustrated. You will work long hours to see your ideas through to completion.

You crave being alone in your own private space, where you can read, think, and escape the world. You especially need to be left alone when you are in a groove. Like some other A's, you may need your work environment to be very comfortable and visually pleasing. Or you may just need your own space, which may be as messy and disorganized as the thousands of thoughts competing for attention in your head. Either way, having your own space is the *only* option.

How Als Relate to Others

Your coworkers or other acquaintances may not understand you or respond to you the way you would like them to. As a result, you often wonder what you have done to turn them off. You may never feel you present yourself as well face to face as you could in your head or in writing.

Because you are creative, intelligent, and idealistic, you can be very critical of the work of others. You enjoy a good debate, because you're convinced you're right and you are eager to convince others.

You love being admired for your talent and intellect. But having a lot of social relationships is hard work for you. You prefer having a small circle of friends who really get you. When you find somebody who fits that description, you're grateful and fiercely loyal.

It may take time and effort to gear up for big events; you have to be in the right mood to socialize or to enjoy (or even tolerate) any attention. You don't mind solitude, as long as it's not for extremely long periods, because you also like exposure to certain activities, mainly intellectual, that stimulate your genius.

The Miscast AI

Like most A's, the work that really fascinates you is in your head, and it involves exploring ideas, experimenting with them, and applying them to new situations. Because AI's are intellectually curious and need to be challenged, any work that involves repetitive tasks is a bad fit. So is highly technical work or anything that involves working directly with customers. If you're an AI in a job that doesn't revolve around exploring and creating, you may find your mind wandering away at every opportunity. Maybe you'll hear a coworker tell a vacation story and let your mind drift into some made-up narrative based on the story. Maybe you'll watch the conduct of the customers or coworkers around you and spend time thinking through your theories about what makes people tick. In any case, AI's are likely to escape from a boring reality by using their imagination.

Of course, many AI's will find themselves driven to create and explore ideas in their spare time. It could be something as simple as keeping a diary, but it could also mean joining a book club or trying to write poetry worthy of publication.

Picture Yourself as an Author

You have a story to share with the world. It might be a story you made up yourself, or it may be a real-life story about something as small as one person's life or something as big as the history of a whole nation. Regardless, telling it will require hard work, a sharp mind, talent, and lots of research (even fiction writers spend many hours researching—or at least the good ones do).

You enjoy writing because you like sharing your knowledge, thoughts, and work with others. Ideas for stories, books, or articles are always popping into your head, sometimes from unlikely places. You filter through them in your mind; a few of them stick and become the start of something you might someday publish.

Getting your foot in the door in the publishing world wasn't easy for you, and you have the rejection letters to prove it. Being a good writer is only part of the recipe for success; being able to market yourself is just as important. Because this does not come naturally, you may need to hire an agent to help you.

There are dozens of ways to work as an author. You can crank out a couple of paperback mysteries a year and make something resembling a decent living. You can write children's books or even teen fiction. You can write textbooks. You can work freelance, penning articles for magazines, newsletters, newspapers, or websites as the opportunity arises. Chances are, you will choose one of these areas as a specialty and dive into it.

There is always an ebb and flow to creating. You alternate periods of fervid inspiration with dry periods when you feel creatively malnourished and need to fill up your tank, maybe by traveling or doing some reading of your own. Writing is not an easy process; you don't sit down at your computer and crank out a novel on the first try. You're always revising and rewriting.

You are most likely surrounded by books and bookshelves, which might overflow onto your desk. You have your computer or a pen and paper always ready, so you can record something of importance at a moment's notice.

Sometimes you get a chance to promote yourself publicly, perhaps speaking to the media or giving talks or book signings. However, these events can be difficult for you, because you need your downtime.

AI Education Requirements

AI jobs usually require at least a bachelor's degree, and many require more extensive education—sometimes a master's degree or even a doctorate. AI's are the perfect candidates for many and (sometimes multiple) liberal arts degrees. They love to learn, read, and study; they are truly lifetime students. Because AI's typically have interests in many liberal arts areas, they often find it difficult to choose a major.

AI Job Opportunities

The challenge for AI's is that there are very few types of AI jobs. Those that do exist usually require some writing and research talent. A sizeable percentage of AI jobs are not standard nine-to-five positions; some involve project work, which means that the job ends when the project is completed or canceled. AI's also gravitate to university campuses because the environment and culture of lifetime learning and a presence of the arts suit them greatly.

In order to find work, an AI usually needs to do lots of networking, have an agent or recruiter, or maybe even create his or her own job, like freelance writing. AI jobs are typically found in metropolitan labor markets, with the exception of positions that can be done electronically.

AI Celebrity

Elizabeth Gilbert, writer

Elizabeth Gilbert is an AI. She is captivating, expressive, and contemplative. Gilbert is a novelist, essayist, short story writer, and biographer; she is well-known for *Eat, Pray, Love: One Woman's Search for Everything Across Italy, India and Indonesia*. This memoir was a chronicle of a year of her spiritual and personal exploration while traveling abroad. The book was on the nonfiction *New York Times* best-seller list for more than a year and was made into a movie starring Julia Roberts.

You were given life; it is your duty (and also your entitlement as a human being) to find something beautiful within life, no matter how slight.

—Elizabeth Gilbert

AS Artistic/Social: The Artistic Nurturer

The AS credo: *I believe every person was born with talent.*
—Maya Angelou

If you're Artistic/Social (AS), you're probably...

- *bohemian.* You may wear Birkenstocks or gypsy outfits. And why not? They're really comfortable.
- *concerned about the environment.* Of course you recycle everything you can. And you are saving up to buy a hybrid.
- *empathetic.* Your friends may call you a "bleeding heart," but you are the first one they run to when they need someone to listen.
- *accepting of other people, cultures, and attitudes.* You feel strongly that people have the right to their own cultures, stories, beliefs, and ways of life.
- *a free spirit.* You've been known to take off in the middle of the night for an unknown destination.
- *a little spacey.* You may get a little distracted from time to time.
- *good-hearted.* You're naturally kind and caring, and it sometimes amazes you that not everyone is.

- *a music lover.* Put on some earphones, plug in your iPod, and you're in heaven.
- *holistic.* You might eat organic food, burn candles, or do yoga every morning.
- *noncompetitive.* You'd rather cooperate (or meditate) than compete for power or money.

The AS Brain

The factors that best characterize the AS, as you might expect based on the Artistic and Social Interest Codes, are a passion for the arts combined with a passion for people. Like the other A CodeCombos, an AS loves to experiment with ideas and appreciates the beauty and depth of good art. But because AS's are so social, they often prefer performance art such as music and theater, and their desire to connect with others makes them natural teachers.

If you're an AS, you have a special blend of talents that allows you to create and perform, as well as to teach and serve. Few performers have the patience or desire to use their creative talents to nurture others artistically, but you delight in it. You love helping people grow. In the high school play, maybe you were more interested in helping the director than being an actor—getting to know all the participants, inspiring them, and coaching them along. In college, maybe you used your interest in arts to expand your social network, participating in activities, such as the choir, the orchestra, and film classes, where you could both practice arts and gather with others who had the same interests.

As an artistic nurturer, you find yourself drawn to service. But not just any service is enough to make you feel fulfilled—you want to nurture people's artistic side. You would jump at the chance to volunteer for a charity that uses art therapy to help traumatized kids. That's the kind of thing we're talking about.

Because of your need to help and interact with others, you do not always reserve enough time for expressing your own artistic talent. As a result, sometimes your efforts to pursue your own artistic development may suffer, and you have many unfinished projects. Because freedom is so important to you, you need independence in what you do. Sometimes you may feel overextended, so your work or study space may be a bit messy. You may have sheets of music everywhere, manuscripts piled high, or art supplies or CDs lying around.

How ASs Relate to Others

The arts are of utmost importance to you, but so are people. You like to encourage others through cards, gifts, scrapbooks, or anything creative and uplifting. You inspire people to follow their dreams.

Because you wear your heart on your sleeve, coworkers and acquaintances can inadvertently hurt your feelings or take advantage of you. However, if you can reel in your sensitivity and understand that most other CodeCombos are not as acutely aware as you, then you can be more tolerant.

Every now and then, the people around you may get discouraged by your laid-back style—some may even consider you flighty—but they still can't help liking you because you are so kind and nurturing.

You see yourself as friend to all, whether they are co-workers, acquaintances, family, or close confidants. However, if you see somebody who is thoughtless or insensitive toward others, this may infuriate you.

David's Story

David came to Jan's office a year after he had graduated from college with a degree in history. His dad was worried about him. He knew David's passion was to become an actor, but he really wanted his son to pick a career that would provide support while he pursued his dream. David's dad was a business owner, and his mom was a counselor. He was the youngest of five children, all of whom had had no struggles in finding a satisfying career path. His parents were perplexed: David was incredibly intelligent, scored extremely well on standardized tests, and was an A student throughout school; they could not understand why he struggled.

When David finished his CareerCode test, he learned that his first code was Artistic and his second code was Social (AS). When Tracy called him to deliver the results of his test, she asked if he had ever thought about substitute teaching. She said that because he was an A, he would be fine with moving from one class to another, as opposed to people with other codes. If he subbed, he could take jobs on the spot instead of having to plan ahead, allowing him to pursue available acting roles. David said he had never considered this type of work, but he did think it would be a great fit for him. He registered with the state and became licensed as a substitute teacher. David's dad thanked us for helping him find such a satisfying secondary path and went on to say that David finished his teaching certificate because he enjoyed subbing so much.

The Miscast AS

As you can surely guess after reading the first part of this chapter, an AS needs creative stimulation to be truly happy, and jobs that are too rigid, too repetitive, or too focused on money or competition are going to be a bad fit. In addition, AS's are bound to suffer in jobs where they can't work with others in a constructive way. Remember, an AS is a nurturer, and that kind of personality trait doesn't lend itself well to working alone.

An AS will always feel drawn to music, performance, and other social kinds of art, so if you're a miscast AS, perhaps you try to satisfy your desire for artistic connection by attending plays or symphonies—or by volunteering to help with your local community theater. Do you still have your high school band flute tucked away in a closet, wishing you had time to play it more? Maybe you love volunteering in your kids' classrooms when they're getting ready for the school play or working on an art project—even if you have to take a few vacation days from your nine-to-five job to do it. For AS's, those kinds of impulses are strong, and they'll usually feel compelled to do something to express them. What they really want, though, is to find a way to express them to make a living.

Picture Yourself as an Art Teacher

Of course, there's no more logical fit for somebody who loves art and loves teaching.

As an art teacher, it's your job to expose your students to the world of art and to get them using their own creativity. Your efforts are aimed not just at those who demonstrate talent. You use art, dance, music, or writing to help your students build relationships, become more confident, and deepen themselves.

When you come across a student whose talent has real potential, you like to make him or her your special project. You're always on the lookout for somebody to take under your wing. You like to check in with your students after they move on so you can see how they are developing.

You relish using creative and unconventional teaching techniques. Your teaching style changes from year to year; in fact, you are never satisfied doing the same program over and over again.

You will work long hours in order to facilitate your school's recital, exhibit, or production. You don't watch the clock, and sometimes you quit only when you are starting to fall asleep. You will run yourself ragged organizing an amazing performance of your students. Your office is probably too small for all of your stuff. Certainly you will custom-decorate your workspace, because it is an expression of who you are. It will be unique, warm, inviting, and passionate, filled with images and words that motivate and inspire you.

If you are a teacher in a public school system, then you always feel like an outsider next to the mainstream teachers—but you wouldn't have it any other way.

You are not motivated by money and may even forget to pick up your paycheck if it is not handed to you. Instead, you live for the chance to nurture people, help them use their creativity and develop their talent, and make sure everyone is the best they can be. You love seeing others express their individuality. You live for the flowers, the applause, and the joy you bring to your audience.

AS Education Requirements

Most AS's complete bachelor's degrees, and you can bet that they spend some time in the fine arts building at whatever college they attend. AS's often earn degrees in arts education and art therapy. Some art therapy programs leading to a license in art, music, or dance therapy require the completion of a master's degree. Some holistic health programs require specific coursework and certification and often a bachelor's (much less often a master's) degree.

AS Job Opportunities

AS's have limited job opportunities. AS jobs are most plentiful and secure in the education field. AS positions in large corporations are often considered expendable and are the first to be cut during lean times.

Some AS's may work as consultants, each establishing their own clientele, rather than finding a traditional job. Most AS jobs require both talent and specific training in teaching or therapy.

AS Celebrity

Bikram Choudhury, yoga guru

Bikram Choudhury is an Indian yoga guru and the founder of Bikram Yoga, also known as Hot Yoga, a series of twenty-six hatha yoga postures that are performed in a hot (105 degree Fahrenheit or greater) environment. In a United Nations–sponsored research project at Tokyo University, Bikram helped doctors prove that yoga regenerates tissues and cures chronic ailments.

> *Come every day for the next three months and I will give you a new body, a new life.*
>
> —Bikram Choudhury

AE Artistic/Enterprising: The Performer

The AE credo: *Leave 'em wanting more.*

If you're Artistic/Enterprising (AE), you're probably…

- *a big spender.* Why not? You only go through life once.
- *a great storyteller.* You're an entertainer at heart.
- *the center of attention.* You always have something to say that everyone needs to hear.
- *conceptual.* You can visualize a project that hasn't even been started.
- *resourceful.* You'll always find a way to get things done.

- *dramatic.* Your life is one big soap opera—and one big soapbox.
- *charismatic.* You are very charming and know how to use it to your advantage.
- *easily bored.* You'll walk out of a party if it's not engaging enough—especially if you're not the center of attention.
- *idealistic.* You know exactly how things should be.
- *impatient.* You don't have the time or patience for slow learners. You want people to play at your level or get out of your way.
- *impulsive.* You'll buy something expensive on the spot if it makes you feel good.
- *eternally optimistic.* In fact, if you wear glasses, they are likely "rose colored."

The AE Brain

If you're an AE, there's no place you'd rather be than in the spotlight. You've always loved to perform, to make presentations, and to capture people's attention with your talent, your wit, or your bold ideas. Applause and accolades are the ultimate payoff for you.

Your life can be a one-person show. You crave attention, and you're one of the few people you know who actually deserves it. You might be a brilliant storyteller, spinning yarns for your friends or your kids, and basking in the glow of their admiration after you've held them enthralled for half an hour. Maybe you shine in the boardroom. No monotone droning and bland PowerPoint presentations for you—only dynamic performances and perfectly delivered laugh lines. Perhaps you live for happy hour, where you can hold court with your friends and keep them laughing (or debating).

An AE's dream job is somewhere in the limelight. Many musicians, comedians, motivational speakers, salespeople, actors, and even politicians fit the description. These varied professions have one thing in common: their goal is to get an audience into the palm of their hand and keep them there.

As an AE, few things are impossible for your creative mind. If you cannot find a way to do something with the resources, people, and skills you have at hand, you will find another way. You are also tenacious: you don't stop until the job is done. You will practice, practice, and practice until you're ready for prime time. You can be very self-critical, seeing errors that no one else notices.

You are a bundle of energy, and you may not slow down or stop until you crash. Then you need your downtime: time alone to reenergize for the next task. You need a lot of stimulation, and you become bored when there is no action. You would rather walk off and be by yourself than remain in a dead environment. You can take yourself to a new high when you are excited about something. You absolutely live for that sensation. You crave being in the limelight, expressing your creativity and autonomy. Performing makes you feel euphoric. An encore performance makes you feel even better.

How AE's Relate to Others

You work best alone—while directing others to do their parts for your project. You're happy to give credit to all members of the team, so long as it puts you on stage to talk about it. Otherwise, you may have moved on to the next project before you think about praising the others who helped you.

You can turn on the charm in a second, but when your creative juices are flowing, or if you're in the wrong mood, others may sometimes need to stay out of your way. You may therefore need someone to serve as a cushion between you and other people you work with. You can also benefit greatly from a personal assistant to keep you on task and on schedule—and to keep your workspace picked up and your projects moving forward.

The Miscast AE

The A in AE stands for Artistic, but that doesn't mean you can just hand an AE a paintbrush and expect him or her to be happy. The Enterprising component of the AE CodeCombo means interacting with an audience, and actively presenting your art or talent is a must. This means many jobs that come to mind when somebody mentions "artistic"—painter, writer, and so forth—are not necessarily good fits.

Likewise, jobs where you don't have much control over your daily projects should raise a big red flag. An AE who is reduced to checking email, processing paperwork, and greeting customers is probably going to be an unhappy AE. So is one who stands at a machine and builds the same products every day or one who spends all day conducting research. Those kinds of tasks are far too predictable and boring for an AE. Because they are drawn to theater, music, and other forms of performance, miscast AE's are very likely to try expressing their creativity in their spare time, playing in a bar band on weekends or participating in the comedy club's amateur night. Almost without fail, the people who do these things would much rather quit their day jobs and find a way to perform for a living.

Picture Yourself in Advertising

Many AE's would love to spend their lives performing—as a musician, comedian, or other performer who works out of a vehicle, traveling from one performance to the next. Some can handle a nomadic life, often by working uninspiring jobs to pay the rent or rooming with like-minded cohorts to save cash. But for an AE who is not interested in that kind of life—or has tried it and is ready to move on—other opportunities await.

The AE brain is a good fit for the advertising field. Many AE's are excellent at coming up with new and exciting ideas for advertising, publicity, or promotion campaigns. It isn't performing, per se, but executing a good advertising campaign is a bit like pulling off a big performance. It's carefully planned, infused with creativity, and meticulously executed. In advertising, you could work in one of two main groups—the account executive side or the creative side. In either role, you'd get a chance to put your big ideas on display and win over an audience.

As an account manager, you are the one pitching ideas to clients and serving as a go-between with the clients and the creative talent. You brainstorm, interpret research, and help plan campaigns. You go in front of clients (or potential clients) and do the big presentation, telling them why your ideas will work and knowing that your company's bottom line rests on convincing them. As each performance or presentation begins, you feel a rush of satisfaction and cannot imagine being anywhere else.

On the creative side, it's your job to contribute your own ideas to the mix and to take it a step further by executing them. Maybe you'll work with a visual artist or script writer or as a director for filmed advertisements used in radio or TV commercials. You have a more hands-on role in making ad campaigns shine for your clients.

Both of these jobs are desk jobs, which might seem like a hard compromise for a pure AE who loves to perform and be in charge. But the chance to be creative and to orchestrate a persuasive campaign can be enough to make an AE feel fulfilled while bringing home a respectable paycheck.

AE Education Requirements

Many AE jobs have no set educational requirements, although advertising jobs usually require a bachelor's degree. The great majority of AE jobs require innate talent more than anything else. Despite this, many AE's are naturally drawn to college because they want to interact with other A's, as well as get involved in campus activities that allow them to direct and perform.

AE's flock to programs in music, theater, speech, and journalism because they like to see performances and promotions. They even like to stand in the crowd at the state fair watching the little man give his spiel to sell potato peelers, because this is a performance with pizzazz.

AE Job Opportunities

There are very few pure AE jobs, and many begin and end with specific projects. Very talented AE's who find the right jobs can earn a great deal, while many others will struggle to earn meager incomes. For those dead set on being a performer, agents and networking are important for finding the next gig.

AE Celebrity

Justin Timberlake, musician, composer, actor, and producer

Justin Timberlake is an AE. Timberlake is charismatic and adventurous. As a young boy he was contestant on *Star Search* and starred in *The New Mickey Mouse Club* TV show. During the 1990s, he was a lead singer with the popular boy band, *NSYNC. He was writer or cowriter of all three singles from *NSYNC's album *Celebrity*, which was certified five-time Platinum by the Recording Industry Association of America. He has released successful solo albums and hit singles, including, "SexyBack." Timberlake began acting in 1999 in the movie *Model Behavior*. Among other movie roles, he portrayed Napster's Sean Parker in *Social Network*. Timberlake launched a clothing line called William Rast, and sponsors a charity golf tournament for the Shriners. Timberland has multiple Grammy and Emmy awards and has made several appearances on NBC's *Saturday Night Live*, *showcasing* his comedic skills.

> *I needed freedom to really express myself.*
> —Justin Timberlake

AC Artistic/Conventional: The Critic

The AC credo: *A critic is a bundle of biases held loosely together by a sense of taste.*

If you're Artistic/Conventional (AC), you're probably…

- *picky.* You set your standards high.
- *methodical.* You're slow, careful, and meticulous. You rarely make mistakes.
- *sharp tongued.* If you're thinking it, you have to say it, even if it stings.
- *protective.* You keep everything you own in mint condition.
- *technical.* Precision is the foundation of your creative process.
- *temperamental.* People accuse you of throwing a tantrum now and then, but you're just expressing yourself.
- *an interpreter.* Your analysis helps others decide if something is worth their time.
- *perceptive and accurate.* Your antennae are always up, and you're very skilled at reading the signals they pick up.
- *cultivated.* You're much more refined than the average Joe.
- *complex.* Because you are both creative and detail oriented, you identify with both Jekyll and Hyde.

- *controversial.* You don't win popularity contests, but you do get people talking. You have strong opinions, and you stand by them.
- *clever.* You deliverer zingers at the speed of light.

The AC Brain

Over time, the word "critical" has somehow acquired negative connotations—but you know better. You understand that "criticism" really means "analysis." The AC has the seemingly contrary tendencies of relishing individual creative expression and demanding that things be done right. The natural intersection of these tendencies is a critical mind: you love art, literature, and the fine things in life, but you aren't interested in settling for less than the best.

If you're an AC, you love theory, parsing, and dissection. Do you like to read critics' reviews before seeing a movie or a play, then debate with your companions on the way home about whether you agree? Some would go to a nice restaurant and order a steak, but you're more likely to pick something adventurous and then delight in analyzing it. Maybe people see you as snooty because you're not shy about ripping into music that isn't original enough for you. (Let them watch *American Idol* if they will, but you're more likely to be found listening to your Sonic Youth CDs from high school). Maybe you can't read a novel or a newspaper (or even an email from a friend) without noting the typos and poorly chosen words—indeed, ACs are often editors of others' words or music.

You might get a thrill out of analyzing F. Scott Fitzgerald's work, or explaining (à la Andy Rooney) why advertising inserts in magazines are so annoying, or demonstrating how Frank Lloyd Wright's designs had an enormous negative influence on architecture.

You have your own unique technique, creative style, and flair. You like puzzles because they combine form with stimulation. When you tackle a new project or topic, you can become bogged down in research or details, but you're nevertheless reliable, a self-starter who is able to meet deadlines. You may be in the middle of several unfinished projects, because you want whatever you do to be perfect. Whether you're writing an essay for a class, preparing a presentation, or making your kids' Halloween costumes, you will spend hours writing and rewriting, sewing and ripping.

You like to have your own studio or office. Because you are the only A CodeCombo who needs order and structure, you must know exactly where everything is in order to work most efficiently. You are highly sensitive to your surroundings and have difficulty working in an area that is not aesthetically pleasant. You need a quiet, nondistracting atmosphere. You also need and like organization, sometimes to the detriment of the project. Because many AC's bead or do fiber arts, you may have a collection of beads, needles, yarn, or other materials in your stash.

How ACs Relate to Others

By nature, you're probably somewhat critical of everyone. This includes your coworkers. You really can't help this, because you're so acutely perceptive and you speak your mind. As a result, others may see you as standoffish, contrary, overbearing, or abrasive. In the ideal situation, this wouldn't be much of a problem for you, though, because you prefer to work independently. Because you are something of a contrarian, you like a good verbal fight involving divergent viewpoints. You're not likely to give in once you've dug in your heels.

Most of all, you don't want to interact with others when you are knee-deep in a project. You feel that doing things right takes a tremendous amount of energy, and it needs to be directed toward your work, not your coworkers.

The Miscast AC

Not only do AC's have a deep desire to create or experience transcendent works that illuminate the human condition or shine a light on the beauty and tragedy of the world, but they also want to see it done right. In a word, they're picky. They like to be part of something great, and they feel compelled to impose order on situations that cry out for it. An AC who ends up in a job where those tendencies are repressed is likely to do what people with high standards do when they're forced to settle for less: get crabby.

If you're an AC, you have a sharp eye for detail, you always want to express your opinion, and you're not likely to abandon your position easily. Sounds like a supervisor's nightmare, doesn't it? If you aren't getting a productive outlet for your need to scrutinize, you probably spend a lot of time directing that energy at your work environment or the people around you. If only they'd just do things your way.

Seeking fulfillment, many ACs will channel their artistic desires and analytical skills into spare-time pursuits. After eight hours of putting up with work—and having to censor

yourself much of the time—you're probably ready to un-
wind. An AC might do this by seeking out the newest and
most talked-about music, theater, or TV shows, enthusias-
tically gobbling it all up, and delighting in picking it apart
with a spouse or some friends. What's overrated? What's
underrated? What secret delights are the masses missing
out on? You never get tired of those kinds of conversations.
And if your job doesn't allow you to play an analytical role,
you'll probably find yourself doing it on your own time in
order to feel contented.

Picture Yourself as a Critic

What else? It's the job that most allows an AC to thrive and
feel fulfilled, because it involves interacting with the creative world as well as dissecting and analyzing it. As a critic,
you're in the business of telling it like it is. Not all art is created equal, and you love experiencing and sharing the news
about the very best of it—but you also revel in pointing out
the glaring flaws of the stuff that's not up to par.

Your job is to decipher, interpret, translate, and examine
one or more art form, craft, or medium. You might write
music reviews for a local newspaper or magazine (only a
select few will find their work in a national medium such
as *Rolling Stone* or Pitchfork.) You might do restaurant reviews for a website or a radio show. Most likely, these days,
you'll work in a mix of media, including print, online, and
broadcast. Your opinions are sought after, even though not
everyone agrees with them.

You see your job as helping to increase others' awareness and understanding. You consider this to be quite a

responsibility. You spend some of your time on research. This gives you an ever-growing technical understanding of the field you love. It's probably a field in which you have a high degree of experience and schooling. It's hard to write a credible review of a Tennessee Williams play or a plate of pad thai unless you know much more about it than the average person. You are stimulated by new works of art, which you can't wait to experience so you can critique and interpret them.

Getting a start in the field is not easy. Often critics must burnish their credentials by writing on a freelance basis for years before building a reputation and getting a bigger gig. Even then, it might be a small media outlet or a junior position with an institution such as a library or museum. Only those with tremendous talent and tenacity rise to the top of the profession. And usually, strong writing skills are absolutely essential. To get your message across, you need to know how to communicate flawlessly.

AC Education Requirements

ACs are drawn to higher education for good reason: nearly all AC jobs require a four-year college degree and years of artistic specialization. Many require a graduate degree in the field.

AC Job Opportunities

AC's are specialists. They are literary critics, film critics, design critics, and food critics, as well as artistic and social commentators who provide their opinions about how things should be done. Writing and research abilities are absolutely essential for AC positions.

There are a variety of AC jobs but a limited number of job opportunities; those that do exist require both artistic talent and expertise. AC's are often employed by universities, libraries, publishers, and the media. The vast majority of these jobs are in major metropolitan areas. Part of getting an AC job involves being in the right place at the right time. Some AC's are self-employed, working from home offices and sending in their work for publication.

AC Celebrity

Carrie Ann Inaba, dancer, choreographer, TV host, and singer

Carrie Ann Inaba is an AC. She is blunt, feisty, and hard to please. She is well known for her appearance as one of three judges on the ABC television series *Dancing With the Stars*. She danced alongside Jennifer Lopez and Madonna back in the 1990s and has choreographed several television series, including *American Idol, So You Think You Can Dance*, and the Miss America Pageant. She studied at Sophia University and the University of California, Irvine, before graduating from the University of California, Los Angeles, with a BA in world arts and cultures.

Precision is your middle name, sister.
—Carrie Ann Inaba

Connect with other "A's" & resources online at
www.CareerCode.com/A

CHAPTER 7

Social (S): The Helpers

There are lessons that most of us learn as children. We discover that a group of people working together can accomplish much more than each could do alone. We see that when we're having a hard time, we need somebody to lean on; we learn that helping others can be one of the most rewarding and satisfying experiences in life.

These are the principles that make a community work. People help each other. They act not just out of self-interest but also out of regard for their family, friends, neighbors, and even strangers. They know that nobody can go it alone and that all of us are required to help, to teach, and to heal to whatever extent we can.

Some people take this aspect of human nature to the extreme and spend their lives doing things to help other people. For them, their work is much more than a job: it's also their contribution to making the world a better place. And they genuinely can't imagine doing anything else.

These are the people described by the S, or Social, Interest Code. They're the teachers, the social workers, the nurses, the community organizers, and the volunteers. They are the ones who tend to other people's minds (psychologists), bodies (doctors), and souls (spiritual leaders). They are the ones who foster the connections between people and use those connections to make the world better.

Getting along with people is second nature for an S, and life—or work—just wouldn't seem right if it were spent alone.

If your first code is S, then you are very likely…

- friendly
- connected
- accepting
- concerned
- loyal
- generous

The S Interest Code

Not every S is a social butterfly, but by definition, they are all social creatures of one sort or another.

You can almost always spot an S, because their outward focus makes them the ones whose Interest Code is most easily observable at first glance. He's the one who volunteers to help at a nursing home while his friends are sleeping in. She's the high school student who somehow rises above all the cliques and makes friends with everybody. It's the person who strikes up a conversation with people in the line at the grocery store and is genuinely interested in their stories.

S's are drawn to environments where they can work closely with and around other people. They get great satisfaction out of enlightening, informing, helping, training, or curing others. They are natural counselors and confidants. They feel valued when people seek them out to discuss personal problems and ask for advice. S's are also natural mediators, since they're not comfortable with conflict or discord.

S's are genuinely team-spirited and collaborative. They need to feel a personal connection to their coworkers and managers in order to do their best work.

S's are positive and supportive, and they want to work in an environment that fosters these qualities. An S will be very uncomfortable in an office where there is a lot of tension.

The mission for an S revolves around service. An S teaches, nurtures, supports, cares for, heals, negotiates with, listens to, advocates for, and cares about people. As teachers, nurses, counselors, and social workers, S's embrace all who enter their care and smooth out the rough edges of life. Regardless of their official job titles, S's consider themselves in the business of people.

How S's Can Get in Trouble

S's often struggle to set boundaries with their coworkers and the people they serve. Because they don't like conflict, they can put off or avoid things that involve discord. Because S's can easily get caught up in interacting with people, they may not get all their paperwork completed. This causes many S's stress and guilt.

S's have high burnout rates because they take on others' problems, tasks, or loads. It's easier and more comfortable for many S's to take on too much than to say no. Sensing this, bosses and coworkers may take advantage of them by overloading them. S's can be indecisive because they want everyone to like them and don't want to take sides. An S can sometimes be so supportive that he or she doesn't challenge others to improve. An S may accept things as they are and fail to push for more, often settling for mediocrity from others.

Education for S's

Because S's value service above all else at work, there is a strong labor market demand for S's of all educational levels. The educational requirements for an S vary greatly from job to job and from CodeCombo to CodeCombo. Some S jobs require no postsecondary training. Many S jobs require a two-year specialist degree or license. Others require a bachelor's degree, and some require a master's degree or more.

S CodeCombos

- SR: The Trainer
- SI: The Specialist
- SA: The Advocate
- SE: The Connector
- SC: The Caretaker

SR Social/Realistic: The Trainer

The SR credo: *Your goals are my commitment.*

If you're Social/Realistic (SR), you're probably…

- *a coach.* If you're not coaching your child's soccer team, you're coaching a coworker on how to be a better golfer.
- *a mentor.* You enjoy helping others develop their skills and relationships.
- *a team player.* You love working together with a group.
- *social.* Every interaction is an opportunity to catch up with other people.
- *a doer.* You don't just hope for change. You're a serious achiever and a go-getter.
- *competitive.* Pushing yourself gives you that adrenaline rush that you live for.
- *persistent.* You believe firmly in preparation and planning—and in carrying out the plan.
- *responsible.* You don't let people down.
- *frank.* You tell it how it is—no sugarcoating.
- *goal oriented.* You have objectives to meet, and you're going to reach them.

The SR Brain

You know those exercise shows on TV, where the muscle-bound man firmly but cheerfully implores you to pick up the pace as he and his supporting cast of workout partners move through an aerobics routine? That guy could be the mascot for SRs.

An SR likes to help motivate, coach, or teach others. SRs are, in a way, natural leaders because they combine the R Interest Code's hands-on focus with the S Interest Code's desire to share knowledge and help others meet goals. Successfully guiding another toward an objective, or leading a team to get there as a group, is the ultimate accomplishment for an SR.

If you're an SR, your mission in life is to help others make better lives for themselves. You believe in hard work, for both yourself and those you work with. It's easy for you to be assertive when you believe others need to be told what to do to improve their lot.

You're the kind of person who believes anything worth doing is worth doing with all your heart. When you tackle a situation, you like to have a structure. People can rely on you to be organized and take charge of a situation—they had better stick to the plan, or you'll have to steer them back on track in a respectful, forceful manner.

Your Social nature may lead you to speak in favor of doing things for the good of others—and may cause frustration when others don't focus the way you do. Your Realistic nature may lead you to join a club or a sports team when you have the opportunity.

You like to work with people, but you also like to incorporate some form of movement or physical activity into your environment. An SR who's a teacher might do this by setting up movement activities for the students and coaching them to meet their goals. Other SRs feel drawn to jobs or activities that are more overtly physical, like athletics and physical therapy.

You're happy when you know you've made a difference in people's lives—a difference you can measure. You also appreciate receiving respect from people you help, whether it's on the job or in your private life, such as when you coach a friend through a problem with their family or teach young kids how to throw a football.

How SR's Relate to Others

You have a soft but reliable side that makes the people you help trust and have faith in you. You like and appreciate teamwork, whether the team has two, ten, or fifty members. In fact, a combination of team spirit and concerted effort make you feel most alive. You expect all team members to pull their own weight.

You have a great sense of team spirit; in fact, you are likely happy when you're playing sports or participating in another team activity. Because you want to see things done with vigor, you're not usually shy about trying to inspire others in a positive way. You can become annoyed when people don't follow your advice, and some of your contacts may see you as being a pest.

The Miscast SR

Bosses talk about teamwork all the time. But much to the chagrin of managers everywhere, employees rarely satisfy every wish of their bosses. So for all the talk of teams, many work environments are characterized by rivalry, backbiting, and (almost worse) indifference.

That's not a good situation for an SR, who feels most fulfilled when people are on the same page and working toward the common good. When teamwork breaks down, an SR may feel out of place and withdraw socially—but he or she may also feel the need to continue challenging people to do better, which will probably lead to frustration. The feeling that other people aren't working as hard as they should and don't care about their coworkers is hard for an SR to swallow. Some SR's who are unhappy at work will try to compensate in their spare time. An obvious way to do this would be by coaching their kids' soccer team, but this need may also be met by volunteering to be a Girl Scout leader or becoming a mentor to a child as a Big Brother or Big Sister.

Picture Yourself as a Physical Therapist

Your job is to help people recover from injury or surgery, build up their strength, and perhaps most importantly, build up their confidence. You're uniquely suited for this job because you're patient, you have the ability to motivate people, and you truly care about helping others. You probably see several clients a day, most likely in an office setting where you keep the tools of your trade, which include not only exercise and therapy equipment but also charts and forms that you use to track progress and outline treatment plans.

Your goal is to help somebody gain the strength they need to function, but your job is not purely to tend to your clients' physical side. You need to be able to size them up quickly and learn what motivates them. You know it's part of your job to push them, but it's also your job to understand their limitations and know when to stop. You like to build up an amiable relationship with your clients, and they are often grateful for your help even long after they stop seeing you on a professional basis. You don't get tired of being around people, even when they are only capable of taking baby steps and need a lot of support—circumstances that could be draining to others. For you, working long and hard pays off when you watch a stroke victim begin to walk.

SR Education Requirements

There is no one-size-fits-all-SRs educational program. Some SR jobs require a high school education (or less), some require the completion of a two-year vocational training program, and some require a four-year degree.

SR Job Opportunities

SR jobs are moderately available. The majority of them are found in the fields of healthcare, education, and protection.

SR Celebrity

Denise Austin, personal trainer

Denise Austin is an SR. She is gregarious, enthusiastic, and energetic. Austin is a fitness instructor, author, columnist, and member of the President's Council on Physical Fitness and Sports. She initially attended the University of Arizona on a gymnastics scholarship and later transferred to California State University, Long Beach, graduating with a degree in physical education and a minor in exercise physiology. Since then, she has been teaching classes, producing fitness shows, creating exercise videos, and writing books on exercising and staying fit.

> *If fitness came in a bottle, everyone would have a great body. Skip the quick fixes; hard work is what ensures lasting results.*
>
> —Denise Austin

SI Social/Investigative: The Specialist

The SI credo: *To growth, to healing, and to life.*

If you're Social/Investigative (SI), you're probably…

- *responsible.* You want to explain the problem and then provide the solution.
- *helpful.* Helping others is what life is about.
- *insightful.* You see things many other people don't—which is why friends and family often ask you for advice.
- *concerned.* Your natural impulse is to be caring and empathetic.
- *supportive.* When a client, coworker, friend, or family member needs a pep talk, you're the one to give it with insight.
- *rational.* You can't afford to be flaky when you've got others' well-being in your hands.
- *tactful.* You've learned how to get your point across without ruffling people's feathers.

- *understanding.* You're an engaged and compassionate listener.
- *perceptive.* You're aware of people's needs, even when they don't express them overtly.
- *inquisitive.* Asking others questions helps you do a better job.
- *systematic.* You understand and trust well-designed processes, and you tend to follow them step by step.
- *a team player.* You enjoy doing what you can to better people's lives.

The SI Brain

An SI combines a strong wish to help people with the intellectual curiosity and ability to do so in ways that most people can't. They are drawn to professions such as medicine, high-level teaching, and psychological therapy, fields that require scholarship as well as a caring social nature.

As you go deeper into this book, you'll notice similarities as well as key differences when you compare each CodeCombo with its inverse. In this case, the SI shares many characteristics with the IS. Both are careful, curious thinkers motivated by a desire to find answers, solve problems, and help people. But because the SI is defined first and foremost by the dominant Social component and the Investigative piece comes second, an SI desires a more hands-on approach to helping others than an IS, who might not mind spending more time with books and data than working directly with people. Using the healthcare field as an example, an SI is more likely to be a hospice nurse than an optometrist, while it's the opposite for an IS.

Like an IS, or most I's for that matter, an SI is largely an intellectual creature, one who devours books and magazines and isn't easily dissuaded by hard-to-solve problems. For an SI, however, the search for information and understanding is more about helping people than it is about creating something original, competing with peers, or mastering a subject for its own sake.

If you're an SI, you've likely been known as curious, bright, and outgoing for most of your life. Maybe as a kid you dreamed of being Nancy Drew, using your keen wit and intelligence to solve problems for other people. When you were in junior high and high school, you were probably in one or more school clubs or after-school activities, and you were one of the kids who came up with the best ideas for fundraisers or prepared a thorough presentation about your group for the school board. You're likely an environmentalist, and you believe learning about the Earth and caring for the world and all its inhabitants as the highest calling and the most fundamental way to help others.

No matter what you study or what you do for a living, being thanked and appreciated by a classmate, a teacher, a client, a customer, or a family member touches your soul. However, with or without their thanks, you are deeply gratified when you are able to help someone, especially when you are able to do it in a life-changing way.

You also appreciate being recognized for your efforts by your employer, provided it is genuine and not just mindless motivation. At work, you get great satisfaction from being part of a team that is working toward a common goal.

You are very approachable and want to help as many people as you can. You enjoy providing a community service, and in fact you may be an enthusiastic volunteer—though you'd prefer to do something challenging, like serve on a nonprofit board of directors, rather than something mindless, like licking envelopes.

How SI's Relate to Others

At times you are content to work independently or one on one with coworkers, peers, or clients. At other times, you work collaboratively. You understand you may take the lead or serve in a supporting role. You're very comfortable in either situation.

Being a highly intelligent and thoughtful person as well as one who values relationships above all else, sharing ideas and feelings with others is important to you. You have most likely developed excellent listening and speaking skills.

You have a strong sense of professionalism and expect the same from your coworkers or classmates. At work, you often befriend your coworkers, but you also need them to understand how important it is for you to have time and space to work and decompress.

It's important for you to be valued by your coworkers for your contribution. You insist on open and honest communication with your coworkers. Sometimes you have to give orders, and sometimes you have to take them. You have no problem being in either position.

The Miscast SI

If you've been reading the other chapters of this book and have familiarized yourself with the I and S Interest Codes, you might already be forming a pretty good idea of the kinds of jobs that are not a match with an SI's skills and interests. A purposeful career and life for an SI is one that first and foremost is about people. But it's not enough just to interact with them on a superficial level. Being a customer service representative, a retail clerk, or a salesperson would provide plenty of interaction with other people, but these types of careers will not provide the intellectual stimulation an SI needs.

An SI who has gone down a career path that isn't fulfilling is more likely than workers with other CodeCombos to reach out and try to find purpose and satisfaction in life's "extracurricular activities," such as volunteering, being part of clubs or organizations, and traveling. The need to meet people, learn about them, and feel good about relationships drives SIs into helping professions, but if it can't be met through work, the SI will passionately pursue those kinds of opportunities outside of work.

Another characteristic of SI's is they're likely to put a lot of effort into family affairs. But it's not enough just to be there for the kids or the extended family—an SI wants to make sure the people in his or her family have the best. Not the best material things, but the best kind of parenting, the best experiences, and the best schools. An SI might spend hours reading and researching these things, as well as talking to others to gather information, in the quest to get it right.

Picture Yourself as a School Psychologist

Your job is to delve deeply into what makes other people tick—not in a cold and clinical way but as an advocate and a helper. The job combines your natural ability to connect with people and your desire to understand and find answers.

People place their trust in you, and you take that trust very seriously. People talk to you about their fears, worries, hopes, successes, and failures, and you pay close attention, filing away the details to help you fill out a mental picture of what is going on inside your clients' heads. You listen patiently, you ask questions, and you carefully read your clients to determine if they need to be consoled or challenged. You know that people are complicated and no two clients will call for the exact same approach.

Helping people to find better self-awareness, conquer the things that are difficult for them, improve their relationships, and generally live a more satisfying life is the ultimate payoff for your work. You see yourself making a difference every day by applying your people skills and your sharp intellect to the problems of others.

Your office is welcoming and well-organized, and you keep detailed charts and records on clients. It's important for you to maintain the right atmosphere in order to make people comfortable—as well as to manage your time efficiently, because as soon as one client leaves, another is on the way.

You keep current with the latest treatment techniques, medical advances, and theories related to your profession. You also have excellent project management skills and use them to design and manage treatment plans.

SI Education Requirements

Nearly all SI jobs require completion of a bachelor's degree, many require a master's degree, and some require an MD or other doctorate. Because SI's are highly specialized, they need advanced training.

SI Job Opportunities

SI's have a variety of job options. Many jobs are well suited to SI interests. Most are in the fields of health, education, and social services. The few promotional opportunities involve advancement within a particular specialty.

SI Celebrity

Ina May Gaskin, midwife

Ina May Gaskin is an SI. She is compassionate, humanitarian, and innovative. Gaskin is a certified professional midwife (CPM) who has been described as "the mother of authentic midwifery." In 1971 Gaskin and her husband founded The Farm in Summertown, Tennessee. There, she and other midwives created The Farm Midwifery Center, one of the first out-of-hospital birth centers in the United States. The Gaskin Maneuver, also called "all fours," is a potentially lifesaving technique Gaskin introduced to modern obstetrics in 1976.

It is important to keep in mind that our bodies must work pretty well, or there wouldn't be so many humans on the planet.

—Ina May Gaskin

SA Social/Artistic: The Advocate

The SA credo: *We make a living by what we get, but we make a life by what we give.*

If you're Social/Artistic (SA), you're probably…

- *talkative.* You love to catch up with people because you are interested in them.
- *a positive thinker.* People who don't know you well sometimes think your optimism isn't genuine, but it is.
- *absentminded.* You admit it: you can easily get sidetracked and forget things.
- *trusting.* You give others the benefit of the doubt—even though you sometimes get burned as a result.
- *forgiving.* You don't hold grudges, and you give great therapy hugs.
- *warm.* You want to be almost everyone's friend, and they usually feel the same way about you.
- *hospitable.* You make everyone who enters your home feel welcome.
- *accepting.* You are nonjudgmental of others; you can see many shades of gray and multiple sides of the same issue.

- *giving.* You'd happily give someone the shirt off your back if someone really needed it.
- *sensitive.* You feel like crying if you see a child or animal get hurt.
- *vulnerable.* Sometimes you wish you were better at setting personal boundaries, so you wouldn't get hurt so often.

The SA Brain

Much of this book has been about how people who fit into each CareerCode find fulfillment in life. Well, when it comes to SA's, one of the ways they find fulfillment is by helping others find fulfillment using creativity and resourcefulness. They prefer flexible environments and may totally lose track of time while interacting with family, friends, students, customers, or clients.

If you're an SA, you feel your mission in life is to encourage others. As soon as you see a need, you volunteer immediately, because you are on this Earth to serve people and your community. Your number one concern is to be as helpful as possible to whomever you are working with. You're an idealist, you believe in the potential of people, and you want to do whatever you can to help them reach it.

Do any of these seem familiar? In elementary school, you were the kid who stood up for the kid who was getting picked on. In high school, you visited a grandparent in a nursing home and greeted the residents with a friendly smile and maybe got to know some of them; many of your peers may have felt awkward or uncomfortable with the elderly, but you knew that people are just people, no matter their age. Later in life, when you heard the county was looking for foster parents, you applied, because the thought of needy kids without stable families almost broke your heart.

When somebody looks to you for guidance or help, you take them seriously. You always strive to act in an honorable and respectful way no matter whom you are dealing with. After all, everyone is created equal. You are very generous, and if you have money, you may be tempted to give much of it away.

You want every day to be "casual day" and to be able to put your feet up on your desk. You like flexible hours and duties, as well as projects that involve imagination and inspiration. Creativity may be more social or conceptual than artistic. Helping and serving others is all-important to you, but you also enjoy being creative and planning activities to help people connect with each other.

You are a natural teacher, mentor, and parent. Money is never your driving force. You would gladly do your job for free. (In fact, many SAs do: they are full-time or long-term volunteers.) A big hug from someone you've helped is a thrilling reward.

How SA's Relate to Others

You routinely place others' needs before your own. This goes for friends, coworkers, children, and, if you're already in a helping profession, your students or patients. You zero in on those who have the greatest need and then spend great amounts of time helping them.

People see you as a giver, always willing to provide a listening ear, lend a hand solving a problem, or give fifty dollars here and there. Not everybody realizes it, but you sometimes do this at the expense of meeting your own needs. But you wouldn't have it any other way.

You are extremely sensitive and understanding with the people you work with or those you work for. If one of them tells you a sad story about themselves, you'll get a genuine lump in your throat. You have great patience and are willing to accept the flaws of others.

You are a nurturer by nature. With your family and friends as well as with coworkers and clients or customers, you're the kind of person toward whom others naturally gravitate. And people feel comfortable opening up to you; they can tell you truly care, even if they can't articulate it or put their finger on why.

You love being nurtured, so you like working with other SA's. But since you seek to understand everyone, you also enjoy the diversity of working with people having other CodeCombos or CareerCodes. Coworkers and peers who require more structure can sometimes get annoyed with your free-form, "touchy-feely" style. They might have trouble understanding you, which kind of irks you, since you want to understand and accept everyone.

The Miscast SA

That free-form style we talked about isn't always considered an asset by employers. You need to be in a relaxed environment where time and productivity aren't carefully watched and measured, so any job where you're expected to punch a clock, account for every minute you spend, or meet strict deadlines is likely to be trouble. To you, work should be a lot like hanging out. You like flexible hours and duties and creative projects to work on.

The standards you set for your own work performance may vary—possibly greatly—from the standards placed on you by your employer. For example, you may feel that even a small amount of progress is worth the immense effort you have devoted to helping another person, while your organization may be very concerned with achieving specific benchmarks.

To an SA, life is about making a difference and getting to know people, and it's hard for an SA to feel fulfilled in a career unless it allows for that opportunity. An SA who works in insurance billing would probably rather be talking to the patients about their problems instead of getting their claims processed; an SA who works as a hairdresser probably values forming relationships with customers more than raking in money for the shop owner.

Picture Yourself as a Nonprofit Worker

There are thousands of nonprofit agencies and groups. For the most part, their employees have a few things in common: they go to work because they want to make a positive difference, they have accepted that they're not going to get rich doing it, and they couldn't imagine life any other way.

An SA might find deep satisfaction working for a charity or an advocacy group, especially if the job offers the chance to help people one on one. A job with a clean-water action group meeting with like-minded citizens, landowners, and government officials could be just the thing to keep an SA engaged in work. It's the kind of job where an idealistic, energetic, social person can thrive. Or how about a job running a food shelf? Meeting people who've fallen on hard times and need a hand up, and doing your part to get them back on their feet, makes you feel you're doing your part to make the world a better place—even if the faces of the kids and the overworked moms can break your heart.

Sometimes you're asked to work long hours, and you are usually glad to devote your extra time to your job, because you know that people rely on you. Your work can be exhilarating, when your organization gets a big grant or when somebody you've helped sends a heartfelt thank-you note, but sometimes it's also frustrating—when it feels as if it's you against the world and you can never help everyone who needs it, and you feel unappreciated. But you soldier on because it matters to you.

You may have a small office or even just a corner desk somewhere, and it's not necessarily well-kept. Your number one concern is to be as helpful as possible to whomever you are working with, even if it means you have to work in clutter. Your workplace may be casual, with employees showing up in jeans and sneakers, but in some cases you're expected to put your best foot forward and wear business attire to work. Either way, you don't care much. Such things are of little concern to you.

Your workspace is free-form. You may have inspirational quotes on your walls. Because you are artistic as well as social, you want your walls decorated so that your workspace feels warm and inviting.

SA Education Requirements

SA's are drawn to four-year colleges (especially those where lots of students live on campus) because they are so very social. They love the experience of college and the opportunity to meet new friends and work as a part of a team. Most SA jobs do require a bachelor's degree. When it comes time to choose a major, most SA's find a natural fit in education or social work, though they may find programs in nonprofit programming or social sciences attractive.

SA Job Opportunities

It is difficult for SA's to find paid employment at more than minimal compensation. Many positions that match their CodeCombo are volunteer positions. Most paid jobs are in education and social services.

For better or worse, SA's are quintessential volunteers. Many give greatly of themselves but are not financially compensated for it.

SA Celebrity

Ron Clark, teacher and advocate

Clark was featured in the made-for-TV movie *The Ron Clark Story* for his year spent as a teacher in Harlem. He is known for his ability to raise test scores by using unique and novel methods that incorporate innovation, creativity, and fifty-five classroom rules. He has appeared on many national TV shows, including *The Oprah Winfrey Show*.

When dealing with children, above all else you must have passion.

—Ron Clark

⟨SE⟩ Social/Enterprising: The Connector

The SE credo: *I am a part of all that I have met.—Alfred Tennyson*

If you're Social/Enterprising (SE), you're probably...

- *community minded.* You love to get involved with a good cause.
- *a natural connector.* You put lots of energy into your personal and group relationships.
- *a guide.* You love to show visitors around your home, your workplace, and your town.
- *a facilitator.* You naturally connect people with each other and with community, social, and educational services.
- *friendly and outgoing.* You're a people magnet: you're attracted to them, and they to you.
- *a sharer.* You're more than willing to trade, lend, or give your possessions, your ideas, or your contacts.
- *averse to confrontation.* You admit that you sometimes ignore things that need to be addressed because you just don't want to deal with conflict.
- *a good listener.* People love to tell you their problems, which works out perfectly because you love to hear them and respond helpfully.

- *a problem solver.* If the problem involves people, you want to make things better, and you can be very creative in your efforts.
- *understanding.* You'd make a great juror. You can see every side of a story.

The SE Brain

You love being out in the world, talking with people, making friends and contacts, getting involved, and being part of exciting things that are happening. The more connections you make, the more satisfied you feel.

Does this sound like you? In elementary school, you were the kid whose name everybody knew, the one who was first to make the acquaintance of the new kid, and the one who usually won the prizes for selling the most candy in the school fundraiser. In high school, you were the one who had more extracurricular activities than would fit on a college application form. In college, you signed up for the student senate and spent hours working behind the scenes to bring an influential speaker to campus or to plan the annual cookout in the quad. You were in a sorority or a fraternity. In general, you've always been comfortable working in a group, or as an intermediary among several groups, to get something done.

Because you are outgoing, conscientious, charming, and interested in others, people look to you for ideas, resources, and connections. You've had a variety of experiences in your life, allowing you to learn a little bit about a lot of subjects, and that makes you an ideal participant in any brainstorming session. For you, the ideas just keep coming.

You don't really enjoy spending a lot of time in one place, especially if it's a confined area, like a cubicle. You'd much rather be on the go, meeting, greeting, connecting, and facilitating. You are thrilled when people see you as generous, dependable, and reliable—which is often. You wouldn't have it any other way.

When someone you helped is successful, you feel great pride. SEs are the kind of people who are thrilled at the chance to be a Big Brother or Big Sister to a kid in need or who readily take a new coworker under their wing and feel great pride in being looked up to as a mentor. You are not motivated solely by material things or making piles of money. In fact, if you make a good amount of money or win a monetary award, you're probably looking around for somebody deserving to share it with.

How SE's Relate to Others

As you've surely learned by now, people with an S Interest Code are people persons. Throw in the Enterprising code, and this CodeCombo combines the people person social tendency with an energetic, outgoing personality. You end up with the kind of person who has more than a thousand friends on Facebook: somebody who seems to know everybody, somebody who always seems to have a friend or a contact who can solve whatever problem comes up.

When a career counselor tells students or clients that "networking" is a good way to get job leads, many people cringe. Shaking hands at chamber of commerce mixers and golf outings? Cold-calling human resources departments to ask about jobs? It's not for everybody. But by the time an

SE starts a job search, he or she may already have a Black-Berry with dozens of contacts gained in just those kinds of situations.

SE's are good people developers as well as one-person outreach organizations. If you're an SE, you often have more people to serve than is humanly possible, although you will do your best to provide for all. This might play out within your family (not just your kids or siblings, but maybe every last cousin), in volunteer work (where it seems you can hardly raise your hand to help out before you're serving on the board), or in your neighborhood (where you organize the National Night Out party or the neighbor-hood garage sale). Because you give so much of yourself, sometimes you get burned out.

Because you are quite a people person, you cannot imagine doing a job where you have limited contact with others. Yet you work fairly independently, with little super-vision. Your coworkers love you because you make them feel valued for their contribution to the organization. As a result, people tend to be very loyal to you.

The Miscast SE

Any SE who ends up in a job that offers limited interaction with other people isn't likely to last long. Because they are among the most outgoing people of all, they naturally gravitate toward work that involves lots of connections with other people.

But it goes deeper. SE's need more than just having contact with people. Working at a customer service counter in a retail store offers plenty of opportunities for interaction, but practically no opportunity to interact with people as equals, to work together to solve meaningful problems, to embark upon exciting projects, or to bring people together in pursuit of a goal.

The need to be "out there" in a community, getting things done and building a social network, means any SE— even one with a job that's a good match—is likely to be involved in community activities, such as planning the city's annual festival or coordinating the PTA fund drive for a new playground, in addition to doing his or her job. An SE who doesn't get fulfillment at work will feel even more compelled to find that kind of satisfaction somewhere else.

If you're an SE in a job that's a bad fit, you'll probably know it. Maybe you frequently spend work time thinking about (or working on) personal projects that seem far more interesting, such as writing emails to family members to plan a reunion or making a list of potential donors for a friend's campaign for city council. Maybe you come home exhausted but feel reinvigorated when you start calling friends to round up people for a charity walk.

Picture Yourself as a Community Relations Coordinator

It's in the best interest of almost every public, private, and nonprofit entity to project a good image to its community, to educate others about what it does, and to respond to questions and complaints as they arise. That's the role of public relations and community relations professionals. The skills and desires so common in SEs are a perfect match with this kind of profession. Community relations requires outgoing, positive, enterprising people who can make lots of connections, get a message out, create excitement, and contain controversy.

Let's say you work in community relations for a large hospital located in a residential neighborhood. Neighbors may be concerned regarding the dangers of ambulances racing down streets. Governmental officials may need to be sold on plans to allow an expansion that doesn't meet the zoning standards for the area. The local media may be pressing for a story about a patient's death. And the hospital's board of directors may need somebody to begin planning its fiftieth anniversary celebration. It may fall to you, your extensive list of contacts, and your ability to work with and persuade people to fulfill the demands of this job. You might hold an open house to meet neighbors, hear their concerns, and pass out safety brochures. You might have meetings with key city staff members and policymakers to pitch the case for the expansion, as well as speak to chamber of commerce luncheons and Rotary Club meetings to build community support. You might negotiate some limited access for a reporter to conduct interviews. And you might lead a committee to plan and promote the anniversary celebration.

To do a more effective job, you need to know people and know what their thoughts and feelings are. So you often show up at golf outings, training sessions, conventions, and anywhere else where you can be out and about, shaking hands and making new contacts.

SE Education Requirements

Most SE's can't wait to attend college, mainly because this is an ideal place for winning friends and connecting with people. In fact, their involvement with other students and campus organizations is as important to them as their studies. It is often difficult for SE's to choose a major, because the jobs they are interested in rarely require specific training or specialized education.

SE Job Opportunities

SE's seem to struggle in the labor market because they feel pulled in two directions, given their interest in both social and enterprising environments. One pathway is toward the more social-oriented industries such as education and hospitality, but they also are attracted to business. The truth is, they can work in any industry, but they have to find the right role, or they will never feel as if they completely fit. If they don't feel a genuine fit, then they cannot do what they do best, which is connect and bring others together.

A moderate amount of SE jobs exist. Most of these involve managing and developing others and/or coordinating and facilitating events and programs. Most SE jobs are in social services, community relations, nonprofit organizations, education, or hospitality.

Many SE's would like to work in more business-related areas, but their work style is not always valued by more conventional business organizations.

SE Celebrity

Maud Ballington Booth, cofounder of Volunteers of America and PTA

Maud Ballington Booth was an SE. She was idealistic, persuasive, and zealous. Booth and her husband, Ballington Booth, established Volunteers of America after leaving their posts with the Salvation Army. She focused her efforts on prison reforms and halfway houses and was instrumental in establishing the parole system. She was a founding member of the National PTA.

> *Go wherever we are needed and do whatever comes to hand.*
>
> —Maud Ballington Booth

SC Social/Conventional: The Caretaker

The SC credo: *Less for self, more for others, enough for all.*

If you're Social/Conventional (SC), you're probably…

- *a team player.* You play your role and have no desire to be the center of attention.
- *a good communicator.* You ask questions and actually listen for the answers.
- *responsible and dependable.* You simply don't let people down. If you say you'll do something, you do it.
- *helpful.* You're by no means a doormat; you just enjoy giving service to others.

- *loyal.* Betrayal is unthinkable to you.
- *a fan of order.* You love to keep things running smoothly.
- *reliable.* You rarely miss a day of work or fail to meet a deadline.
- *respectful of authority.* Of course people should respect elders, superiors, and people in charge.
- *trustworthy.* You wouldn't even steal a roll of tape from your employer.
- *hospitable.* You greet your guests at the door and always make them feel welcome.

The SC Brain

An SC is the kind of person who loves to have people over for dinner, but makes sure that every rule of etiquette is followed; the kind of person who enjoyed playing multiplayer games as a child but was as stickler for the rules; the kind of person who can be a warm and friendly parent while also being firm and clear when it comes to keeping rooms clean and following household rules.

Lots of people whose dominant Interest Code is S are kind, well-intentioned, outgoing, and reliable people who need to interact with others to feel happy. SC's are no exception, but they come with a twist: they have a keen awareness of the social contracts and rules that govern interaction, as well as the conventions of businesses and organizations that keep things working smoothly.

For example, SC's would excel at working behind a hotel counter, not only because they'd enjoy meeting people from all over the world and making them feel at home, but also because they'd always remember to keep the keys perfectly organized, make sure the counter is clean and straightened, and ensure that every form is filled out correctly and filed in exactly the right place. An SC is somebody who'd love to work with students and would feel tremendous pride and fulfillment when a pupil succeeds, but would also be known as a teacher who always has a seating chart, insists on clean and legible handwriting, and never lets class out even a minute early.

If you're an SC, you can be trusted with extremely sensitive information, and you are extremely loyal to your organization and your boss. Because of this loyalty and your desire to do everything correctly, you use caution when presented with a new or unusual situation, and you may need to ask for guidance or assistance. You don't want to make mistakes.

You are great at memorizing facts, and you feel most comfortable when you are given specific procedures to follow. You do your best work when you have adequate time to understand the situation, chart the important details, and outline the steps you need to take.

Your attention to detail and positive attitude enable you to perform consistently and keeps the organization running smoothly. You take pride in serving humanity and helping others navigate the unknown. You are a genuine service person. You know that your winning combination is your efficiency with job tasks as well as your warm and welcoming spirit in the workplace.

How SC's Relate to Others

SC's are courteous, thoughtful, and considerate, and they expect the same from others. They are likely to be fiercely loyal to people who meet their expectations, but they sometimes lack patience for people who slack off or bend the rules.

If you're an SC, you enjoy pleasing others. A compliment can be enough to keep you going for days, and knowing that you're appreciated helps you feel you have a purpose. While you like to help, you are wary of being taken advantage of. You want to be valued for your contribution, not taken for granted.

You enjoy having your hands in everything. You want to know what's going on with all the people around you; it helps you feel like you have a good grasp on the social dynamics and the pecking order in your social group, your workplace, or your family. When you understand what makes an organization work and what makes people tick, you can position yourself as a go-to person when a problem needs to be solved, and that's a position you relish.

Professionally, you may be well suited to be a liaison between an organization and the public—the greeter, the gatekeeper, the receptionist, the cashier. You have a good combination of public relations and clerical skills that could be used to welcome customers, discuss problems, and set appointments. You are especially skilled in resolving difficulties with clients.

Your coworkers love you because you are kind and keep them informed and involved, and people usually respect your organizational skills and work ethic.

Anna's Story

Anna went to college thinking she would become a math teacher like her dad. During her first semester she realized there were many other options, and she struggled to find her fit. She was the kind of friend many other students would go to when they needed advice. She was the person in the sorority who always wrote things down and knew meeting times and locations. She selected a major in communication with a minor in math and focused on a career in the insurance business after graduation. Then she married and moved from a city to a rural community in Kansas, leaving her with few employment options.

She called her college friend Tracy to ask for help in finding suitable jobs within a rural area. Tracy tested Anna and learned her codes were SC, Social and Conventional. She sent Anna a list of the qualities of an SC, along with some job selections, and suggested that she look into administrative assistant positions. Anna was relieved to have her codes validated. She was hesitant to work in an administrative assistant position because she felt that she was overeducated to pursue that kind of job, but ultimately she knew she would enjoy doing office tasks and helping to keep an organization running smoothly.

The Miscast SC

An SC is usually best in a job where there are clearly defined protocols and expectations. Nebulous goals and an unstructured workplace make SC's feel uneasy because they need to constantly know that things are working the way they're supposed to and they prefer to be told how things should be done rather than set their own parameters.

So while SC's prefer to work with people, they are not usually cut out for management positions where they are expected to set the tone and the standards and where they might have to deal with unforeseen circumstances. One exception may be middle management, where an SC can take directives from higher-ups and be an effective enforcer for the employees.

SC's have many positive traits, but their brains most often aren't wired for highly creative thinking. An SC isn't likely to be the kind of idea person who would succeed as an entrepreneur or as a designer. Rather, the SC is the person the entrepreneur hires to handle the details and interact with customers, or the person who deals with the designer's clients and makes sure deadlines are met.

A job without a lot of structure is a bad fit for an SC and will probably result in anxiety. And like others with S Interest Codes, SC's are not likely to be happy in jobs that isolate them from other people or expect them to work with their hands.

Picture Yourself as a Caseworker

Your challenge is to get to know a caseload of clients quickly, figure out how to motivate them, and connect them with assistance to get their lives on track. It's your job to help them, but it's also your charge to make them responsible for the decisions they make and the actions they take. Your job requires compassion, but it also requires you to be tough and to stick closely to the laws or procedures that govern your interaction with your clients.

It's your job to create plans with clients. You meet them in your office as well as visit their homes and workplaces, assessing not only their ability to succeed but also the community support systems they have. When appropriate, you direct them to resources for counseling, be it for chemical dependency, mental health matters, or other issues.

Your job requires strong personal boundaries. You need to get to know people whose circumstances are difficult and gain their trust, but you can't be a softy; you must make it clear that you're in a position of authority and that you're willing to help but not to get too personally involved.

You are typically accountable to a government or non-profit agency, and you need to submit reports about client progress. You may also spend time investigating and recommending community resources. This requires organization, discipline, and the ability to apply professional practices to every situation. It certainly isn't a job for everybody, but it's a good fit for an SC because it requires social skills as well as a logical and disciplined mind.

SC Education Requirements

Educational paths vary for the SC because there are so many SC jobs. However, most SC positions require either a two-year or a four-year degree. Some SCs need a graduate degree.

SC Job Opportunities

SC skills—and the SC's caring and organized approach to life and work—are needed in a great many jobs in a wide range of fields, especially hospitality, business, medicine/ health, education, and personal care.

SC Celebrity

Annie Sullivan, teacher and governess

Annie Sullivan was an SC. She was dedicated, nurturing, and effectual—best known as the instructor and companion of Helen Keller. In 1887, when Helen was six years old, Sullivan moved in and acted as her governess. She began teaching Keller language by signing nouns into the girl's palm. She used the sign language alphabet developed by Spanish monks in medieval times.

> *I have thought about it a great deal, and the more I think, the more certain I am that obedience is the gateway through which knowledge, yes, and love, too, enter the mind of the child.*
>
> —Anne Sullivan

Connect with other "S's" & resources online at
www.CareerCode.com/S

CHAPTER 8

Enterprising (E): The Persuaders

People come up with thousands of great ideas every day. But most of these brainstorms won't go anywhere unless a savvy person can sell them. A struggling company may have an opportunity to embrace a new technology and turn things around, but without upper management that can sell the plan to the board, Wall Street, and the employees, the opportunity may pass. A political candidate might have the best platform and the best background, but it'll be impossible to get elected without the ability to persuade voters.

Other Interest Codes are well suited to conceptualize the ideas, do the research, coach the employees, mind the finances, or build the products. But the Es are the ones who get a thrill from making the deals, closing the sales, winning the court cases, raising the capital, planning the corporate strategies, and convincing the voters. They may most easily be understood as natural salespeople—whether they're selling widgets, information, or ideas. But that's not the end of the story. Far from just selling and profiting from the concepts and products invented by somebody else, they are a creative force in their own right. At their best, E's are the calculated risk takers who can shape the way businesses and other institutions work. They are the power brokers who can break down the barriers to progress and bring divergent interests together in pursuit of a common goal.

As with all Interest Codes, there can be a troublesome side to Es. When they're going after what they want, you probably don't want to be the person standing in the way. They can be good at making enemies as well as making deals. They can be workaholics, which is great if you're their employer but not so hot if you're their family. And they're not often the reflective types who decide what should and shouldn't be—they're more concerned with what *can* be, especially if a profit can be had.

If your first code is E, then you are very likely...

- dominant
- persuasive
- outgoing
- competitive
- optimistic
- ambitious

The E Interest Code

E's tend to be intensely productive and goal oriented. They are especially interested and effective at persuading others, and their efforts are most often applied to coworkers and customers.

E's exude power and charisma; when an E walks in the room, everybody takes note. And Es take charge. An E is a leader, a manager, and a salesperson all in one.

E's see the big picture and the largest goal; they want to direct others to get there. They are also natural risk takers. "Nothing ventured, nothing gained" is a credo they can get behind.

The thrill of the chase—whether it's the pursuit of a sale, a new customer, or a personal goal—is a big motivator for E's. Socially, E's tend to be competitive and exclusive. They'd much rather associate with other powerful Es than spend time with people they consider boring, which, frankly, might be almost everybody else. At a party, E's are not likely to spend time talking to everybody; they're more likely to single out somebody who seems popular or influential and gravitate in that direction.

E's are driven to earn as much as they can, which is why so many E's are in jobs and fields that pay commissions. Career advancement is very important to E's. They crave leadership and managerial positions, but because they are also very motivated by money, some E's will turn down a promotion if they feel they can make more money in commissions or bonuses by staying right where they are.

How E's Can Get in Trouble

E's can be volatile because of the constant pressure they feel to achieve and succeed. They never really relax, because they are always pursuing some goal.

Tact is not typically an E's long suit; in fact, E's can become too intense and demanding, sometimes overpowering and intimidating others. And often those with Enterprising personalities are uninterested in what others have to say; they've decided what they want, and there's not much use trying to talk them out of it.

Some E's are pushy by nature, needing above all to get their way. In fact, E's will sometimes compromise their own ethics to reach their goals. When someone says, "It's my way or the highway," that is probably an E.

The things that make some E's so successful can be the same things that lead to their downfall. They can have tunnel vision and may be driven by short-term gain without considering long-term consequences. This can be a double-edged sword: The E way of doing things can lead to great success, such as when visionary entrepreneurs built a technology empire in Silicon Valley and a financial empire on Wall Street. But it can also lead to serious problems, such as when the excesses of tech companies led to the bursting of the dot-com bubble or when the reckless practices of financial companies brought on the economic collapse of 2008.

Education for E's

Many sales jobs require nothing more than on-the-job training or short-term specialized training, such as a real estate licensure course. Marketing and advertising jobs usually require somewhat more training—either a four-year degree or a specialized training program running eighteen months to two years.

E's who aspire to become leaders in business need bachelor's degrees. These are essential to climbing the management ladder. Es who want to become city managers, school administrators, and other such hands-on leaders may need to complete specialized graduate programs as well.

Because E's are so focused on productivity, they usually sit still for only as much education or training as they absolutely need. They want to get out into the market and persuade, sell, or lead as quickly as possible.

E CodeCombos

- ER: The Broker
- EI: The Strategist
- EA: The Promoter
- ES: The Ambassador
- EC: The Director

ER **Enterprising/Realistic: The Broker**

The ER credo: *Go big, or go home!*

If you're Enterprising/Realistic (ER), you're probably…

- *a natural-born leader.* Think Donald Trump.
- *a powerful negotiator.* To you, no is just one step closer to yes.
- *a great salesperson.* You really could sell snow to an Eskimo—and would if the commission was right.
- *influential.* You've got VIP written all over you.
- *blunt.* Tact is for diplomats.

- *forceful.* You pride yourself on being able to get anyone to do anything.
- *a power seeker.* Power and control thrill you. They're also the keys to getting what you want.
- *a workaholic.* Your business radar runs nonstop, even at your kid's soccer game.
- *confrontational.* You're not afraid to butt heads with anyone—especially when they stand in your way.
- *confident.* You never wonder where you stand with others, because you don't care.
- *courageous.* You take risks others won't.

The ER Brain

An ER is the kind of person who's often described as "motivated." ER's see the things they want and go after them until they've reached their goal. Giving up is not an option. But acquiring something you want usually means getting it from somebody else, and that means you'll have to make a deal. And deal making is an art at which ER's thrive, in no small part because they're persistent and confident enough to pursue their goal even when the odds are against them.

An ER might savor the experience of buying a new car or a new TV, looking forward to the chance to match wits with a salesperson and get the best deal possible. Some people would just pay the sticker price, not wanting to be confrontational. But to an ER, everything's negotiable.

Because there's always an objective to achieve, ERs don't feel they have time to waste. They prefer to cut to the chase, with all activities directed toward the big picture or big deal.

The game Monopoly was invented for ER's, because the object is to strategize and negotiate deals in order to acquire more, earn more, climb to the next plateau, and ultimately annihilate your competition. (Similarly, all the different versions of Monopoly that are now available, from Dog-Opoly to NASCAR Monopoly, were probably invented by ER's, who are always looking for new ways to sell something.)

How ERs Relate to Others

If you're an ER, you primarily prefer associations with other ER's, because it is in their presence where deals are made. You also like being connected to others who have similar energy and ambitions.

When they're working, ER's can be so focused on a task that they appear unconcerned about what other people are doing or thinking. This can give them a reputation as brusque or unfeeling. It's not that they're unfriendly; they're just not particularly chatty. On the job, an ER is social only to the extent that it's necessary to grease the wheels of deal making.

That doesn't mean that ER's aren't social creatures. They just draw a clear line between their social lives and their work lives. Their boundaries are apparent. Whether it's at work or in their free time, ER's tend to have strong communication skills. That can help them accentuate their strengths and hide their weaknesses.

The Miscast ER

If you're an ER, you're impatient when you're not in control. When you have to carry out somebody else's explicit instructions, you're likely to second-guess them. And when your job doesn't allow you to get out and make things happen—and distinguish yourself as more successful than your colleagues or competitors—you tend to lose interest.

In a job that's a poor fit, you might constantly find yourself annoyed that the boss or coworkers aren't doing things the way you think they should. Alternately, you go through periods where you lose interest and "phone it in." Working collaboratively isn't really your style, and if you have to spend hours a day working along with a team or sitting through meetings, you'll want to pull your hair out. You'd rather be given a set of goals to go after and then be allowed to head off on your own to strategize and get to work.

You're not likely to thrive in a job where you're at somebody's beck and call. Answering the phones in an office, working behind a customer service counter, or serving as somebody else's support staff is not for you; those jobs would make you feel like a lackey. You have the people skills to succeed in working with customers, and you know to treat them right. But unless you're brokering the deal and achieving tangible results by accumulating sales, you'll feel as if you're treading water and not accomplishing anything.

Picture Yourself as a Broker

It doesn't really matter what you're selling; once you have the job and know the product or service, you're ready to go. You know that your job is to fill a need. Your employer offers something that people want. They just may not know they want it yet, and it's your job to show them. This is a task you approach with zeal.

Some of your time may be spent in an office on the phone, setting up appointments or checking in with customers, but it's probably a bare-bones office with a phone, a place to plug in your laptop, and a bunch of business cards. More of your time is spent pounding the pavement, personally calling on customers or would-be customers.

Sometimes you find yourself dealing with skeptical receptionists and busy clients, but you aren't fazed. You have a mission, and you're going to do everything you can to complete it. If you can just get a few minutes of somebody's time, you're convinced you can close the deal.

Others see you as a workaholic because you spend long hours at your job. In fact, the start and end of your work day are nebulous, because you are often involved in networking activities before, during, and after work—prayer breakfasts, Rotary luncheons, tee times at the club, and racquetball contests.

You feel good when you're setting your own schedule, carrying out your own plans, and getting things done. As far as you're concerned, as long as you deliver the results, nobody's in a position to tell you how to do your job, and that's the way you like it.

ER Education Requirements

Because so many ER's show their entrepreneurial spirit at a young age, they often go straight to full-time work right after high school (or even sooner). In particular, ER's who work in industrial, manufacturing, and transportation fields rarely need college degrees to negotiate and deal. Using their ER traits, they will find a way to network into the job.

Some ER's do find value in a four-year degree, however, especially if they complete a business program at a notable school. With or without formal training or college degrees, ER's manage to find their places in the business world where they can test against the best.

ER Job Opportunities

Some ER jobs are accessed by educational accomplishments, some by work experience. Most of these positions involve selling products, services, and/or ideas; supervising workers; or occasionally doing both. Since ER's are so good at selling and brokering, they have little difficulty finding employment. Some ER's are self-employed, creating their own jobs by offering consultant or agent services.

ER's have no difficulty leaving one job for a better opportunity or pressuring their current bosses to raise their salaries so they don't leave for a better offer elsewhere. In fact, ER's who leave one job may have several other opportunities waiting for them, perhaps working for a former client who was impressed by their abilities. Some ER's have a second job, selling something else—timeshares, shoes, life insurance, almost anything—for a business venture they personally own.

ER Celebrity

Donald Trump, real estate developer and business magnate

Donald Trump is an ER. He is competitive, aggressive, and demanding. Trump is the CEO of the Trump Organization, a US-based real estate development company. He is also the founder of Trump Entertainment Resorts, which operates numerous casinos and hotels worldwide. His extravagant lifestyle and outspoken personality have made him a celebrity for a long time, especially after the success of his NBC reality show, *The Apprentice.*

> *When somebody challenges you, fight back. Be brutal, be tough.*
>
> —Donald Trump

⊞ Enterprising/Investigative: The Strategist
The EI credo: *Don't confuse effort with results.*

If you're Enterprising/Investigative (EI), you're probably…

- *a visionary.* You can see the big picture and the final goal—and lead others to achieve it.
- *ambitious.* You're in the game to win.
- *a planner.* As you always tell people, if you fail to plan, you plan to fail.
- *demanding.* You have to take control if you're going to win.
- *agenda oriented.* After all, profit is not a dirty word.

- *logical.* There are certain steps that need to be taken, in a certain order.
- *organized.* You know how to put all the pieces together to make them work in sync.
- *persuasive.* Part of getting things done is convincing others that you have the whole process figured out.
- *self-confident.* If you don't have confidence in yourself, nobody else will.
- *take charge.* Someone's got to steer the ship, and you're that someone.
- *slightly abrasive at times.* You're never rude just to be rude. But it's often necessary to push people to get the right results.
- *a salesperson.* You rarely miss a trade show.
- *an executer.* You enjoy accomplishing the mission, especially when you lead the charge.

The EI Brain

The EI brain is one that knows no boundaries. If it can be imagined, it can be done, as long as you're willing to roll up your sleeves and work hard on a plan.

You're an intense mix: part strategist, part visionary, and part workhorse. The best military generals have those kinds of EI tendencies. Think of Ulysses S. Grant or Napoleon Bonaparte: bold, confident, and forward-thinking, able to see the big picture as well as orchestrate every last detail of a plan to exploit an opponent's weakness—and stick with the plan even if the early returns are discouraging. They reshaped nations and even continents, and the best and brightest EI's have ambitions on the same scale.

An EI has the methodical nature and inquisitiveness of a researcher, combined with the risk-taking nature and opportunism of an entrepreneur. To an EI, learning a subject forward and backward is a worthy (and attainable) goal, but most EI's don't have any interest in compiling that kind of knowledge and following somebody else's directions about how to use it. More likely, they see the depth of their knowledge as their own personal toolbox, to be used to further their own goals and position in life.

Money, power, recognition, and winning are big motivators for you. When you think about what you want to do with your life, you think big: you want to rise to the top, be known as the best at what you do, be respected and sought after. Your Enterprising and Investigative natures can't help but manifest themselves in the things you do. People think you'd make a good consultant because when somebody has a problem, you're very good at sizing up the situation, gathering the information you need, and finding a solution.

Of course, you also apply these abilities to your own tasks. Perhaps when you started looking for a college, you were the first among your friends to have a short list of top schools researched and compiled, and then you dove headfirst into the process of promoting yourself to colleges, using your finely tuned résumé to sell yourself. Chances are, you weren't satisfied unless you got one of your top choices.

You love to be involved in make-or-break decisions. You also get a rush out of planning and implementing a project that changes the game—or an entire industry. When your employer is looking for people to work on a new initiative, you're the first to raise your hand and you quickly take ownership of the project.

How EI's Relate to Others

Your combination of high intellect and excellent communication can be your best friend or your worst enemy. You are frank and tell it how it is, even if you must be the bearer of bad news.

You may step on some toes, but not because you're mean-spirited. You just do what you have to in order to follow your plan and get the necessary results. You know you won't win any popularity contests, but you're okay with that, because you're in the game to win.

In terms of their relationships with coworkers, EI's differ greatly from job to job, company to company, and industry to industry. Many EI's work independently. Others hire their own small staff, with each player fulfilling some very specific roles and responsibilities. In jobs that aren't EI careers, per se, an EI will tend to distrust coworkers until they've proven they can be relied on and may look upon others as subordinates even when they're technically equals. Once EI's work themselves into upper management, they will usually avoid interacting with lower-level employees, with the exception of their own office support staff.

Some coworkers may see EI's as arrogant and condescending. This doesn't bother EI's. They are far too busy strategizing and planning to worry about what others think of them. To an EI, it's the results that matter, and even if people don't like the person, they'll have to respect the results.

Wally's Story

In a society that values earning lots of money, it's no wonder that a lot of people get into sales but aren't always cut out for it. Wally went to college to study math and economics but ended up quitting before he finished his degree. He took some technical training and found his first job selling computers to small businesses. He loved informing small businesses about how computers and software could help them become more efficient. Wally was successful at this sales job because computers were in demand and he was knowledgeable about the product. He did not really have to sell as much as help his customers with the technical aspects of the product, the kind of help many of them needed. After his success with computers, Wally decided he could sell software, which provided higher commissions.

Software sales turned out to be more difficult. For one, there were many competitive products. Again, Wally enjoyed talking to people about the intricacies of his software product, but he did not enjoy having to make the many cold calls necessary in order to get the product in front of people. Before we tested Wally, he shared with us that he was certain that Enterprising was his first code; he was surprised to learn his results showed his top code was Investigative. He was an IE, Investigative and Enterprising. This explained why he enjoyed selling a tangible, in-demand product with a smaller market base, rather than having to figure out how to get into multiple doors to sell a more competitive product. Wally was relieved to know the kind of sales job that was the best fit for him, so he no longer had to experience failure and rejection in a job that required more E than he had.

The Miscast EI

An EI who's stuck in the wrong job won't suffer it well. The EI brain needs to feel in control, challenged, and properly appreciated. If these needs aren't met, an EI will be extraordinarily restless.

Probably the thing that would chafe EI's the most is a lack of freedom. If you're an EI, a job where you're at somebody else's beck and call will seem like indentured servitude. You need to be able to pursue your own ideas and do it your way. An EI might be able to handle assembling widgets or running a cash register for a few summers during college, but something so mindless would be poison over a sustained period. Same for sitting at a computer all day, working with picky customers, trying to teach somebody, or putting together reams of reports on some project you couldn't care less about.

Some CodeCombos might simmer or suffer silently, but an EI is more likely to be outspoken. Coworkers and supervisors will get the unmistakable impression that the job is a poor fit, and chances are the employment won't last particularly long.

Miscast EI's can find themselves bounced around, getting more frustrated with each stop, until they discover the satisfying sense of purpose that comes with being a bold capitalist adventurer.

If you're an EI, you can't turn off your sharp analytical mind and thirst for knowledge. You know that knowledge is power, and you're always accumulating it in hopes of using it when the time arises. You can't help but notice the opportunities to do things better, to make sweeping changes, and to correct wrongheaded ways of doing things. But if you're not in charge—or unless you have the ear and trust of people in power—you don't get to see those ideas through, and the missed chances will be frustrating.

Picture Yourself as a Corporate Strategist

The jobs come with many different titles: vice president of strategic initiatives, consultant, even CEO. The job title isn't really important, though—what you're interested in is the opportunity. You have a great nose for sniffing out opportunity. You can walk into a struggling business and convince the owner that you can double his gross in a year and that he should hire you on the spot. You tell him, "I'll take a low salary now and grow your business, if you'll give me a percentage of your increased profits."

You can be found in the company boardroom—or, at the very least, near a whiteboard, where you are busy strategizing and sketching out the plan. Because new projects stimulate you, your workspace is wherever that project is being planned or implemented. That's you with the briefcase, the notebook computer, the BlackBerry, and the yellow pad.

You use your personal power and considerable knowledge to energize your organization's workforce. You can walk into a company on your first day and remake it in your image before anyone knows what hit them. These qualities, combined with your high expectations and your relentless focus on results, results, results, can cause some people to quit. You're fine with this. Your greatest thrill comes from developing and implementing a plan that works exactly the way you predicted, producing big profits.

EI Education Requirements

Because EI's want to be experts in their fields, many earn bachelor's degrees. Some go on to specialize in specific niches of business with master's degrees in business, economics, or finance. Some EIs don't earn advanced degrees. Whether or not EI's are formally trained, they usually find their way to the top of the heap.

EI Job Opportunities

EI's do very well in technology-driven fields. They usually have no difficulty entering the labor market, changing jobs, or moving up, in many cases to upper management. However, EI jobs are not as plentiful as sales jobs, since every organization needs fewer leaders than followers.

EI's often find their places in start-up ventures, many of which prove to be quite successful. Other EI's elect to make their own jobs by starting their own companies; turning them into healthy, profitable organizations; selling them for large chunks of cash; and moving on to their next projects.

EI Celebrity

Steve Jobs, inventor, business magnate, and cofounder/ CEO of Apple

Steve Jobs was an EI. He was persuasive, intense, and revolutionary. Jobs designed, developed, and marketed some of the first commercially successful lines of personal computers, the Apple II series and, later, the Macintosh. Driving forward the development of products that are both functional and elegant earned him a devoted following. He believed that great things are done in business by a team of people.

Innovation distinguishes between a leader and a follower.
—Steve Jobs

EA Enterprising/Artistic: The Promoter

The EA credo: *Anything you can imagine can be made real.*

If you're Enterprising/Artistic (EA), you're probably...

- *a natural marketer.* You're always on the verge of making a million.
- *ambitious.* You're going to end up at the top, no matter what it takes.
- *slightly arrogant.* You're valuable, and you know it. If others see that as arrogance, that's their problem.
- *charismatic.* You can be charming and draw people in, especially when you need to get them on board.
- *competitive.* No one's going to upstage or outmaneuver you.
- *a visionary.* You always see the big picture, and you can sell a project that hasn't even been started yet.
- *idealistic.* You're a dreamer, and you can visualize grand plans in exquisite detail.

- *expressive.* You will strut into a meeting, wearing your leopard print skirt or your bright pink dress shirt.
- *high energy.* You're revved up from when your head leaves the pillow in the morning until you lie down again at night.
- *loud and boisterous.* You can't help it that you get loud when you are excited—and that sometimes means you also get asked to keep it down in restaurants.
- *a rule bender.* Rules are really just suggestions, right?
- *an initiative taker.* You don't wait for other people. You just jump in and take control.

The EA Brain

The EA brain goes against the grain and combines a pair of traits that more often than not are in conflict with each other: an appreciation and talent for the artistic side of life and the ability to see the dollar signs in every situation.

An EA is dynamic, energetic, and full of ideas. For an EA, it's hard to think about anything without thinking big. Think of a literary agent, a concert promoter, or a theater producer. These people know their business and love to be in the know about what's going on. They have connections with people throughout their industry. They immerse themselves in the business and love to keep tabs on what others are doing. They can recognize a good thing when they see it. And when they get the chance, they'll throw themselves completely into a project, doing whatever they can to make sure it succeeds—whether it's working the phones late into the night, putting in extra hours to strategize, or running the details through their minds as they shower or shop, hoping for a burst of inspiration.

If you're an EA, that kind of thing sounds like your cup of tea. You love ideas, you love to be part of exciting new things, and you love success. You get a huge thrill from pulling off a big production or event, whether it's the high school musical or the family reunion. But until you work your way up, you might feel a bit restless, always wishing you were doing bigger or better things.

You are a super-achiever—not always because you're the smartest person in the room, but because you do everything with a passion and you're keenly observant. You are multitalented, have boundless energy, and are able to juggle many projects simultaneously.

You are expressive, and you want to dress in a way that befits what inspires you or what you're working on, not the norms of where you work or go to school. You like attention and thrive on getting accolades for your work. You can easily be the star. Your satisfaction also comes from directing the show.

You love being a part of the A-list, attending parties and touching shoulders with popular or fascinating people. You want to be seen at that very important party, and you want to be able to tell your jealous friends about it later. You like money, especially as it pertains to being able to do what you want and move into the right circle of people.

How EA's Relate to Others

When you are feeling passionate about what you're doing, your charisma can be a huge motivator for the people around you, communicating your idealism and vision with enthusiasm and energy. People say your enthusiasm is infectious, and everybody wants you to be in their work group in class or their department at work.

But if you are feeling frustrated, people learn quickly that you can be temperamental and difficult to work with. You might get huffy if things don't go the way you want, or if you wind up butting heads with somebody who's too stubborn to see things your way, or if your ideas don't turn out they way you'd hoped. You know you can be harsh sometimes, and it doesn't bother you. You don't feel the need to apologize for telling it like it is.

When you're working with a group of other artistic people, you expect artistic perfection from everyone, because you want the results to be the very best. But artistic people often have different visions and ideas, so it can be tricky to get on the same page. You are willing to let your collaborators have some space to let their creativity bloom, but you also won't hesitate to rein them in if they start straying too far from the plan.

Socially, you probably have a large network of contacts. When you're around others, you tend to be flamboyant. You enjoy dropping names, and you always have a new story to tell. You love celebrating and living it up.

The Miscast EA

There are a moderate number of EA jobs available; however, most of these jobs require years of work experience, and almost all of them are accessed through climbing the ladder or having raw talent. Be ready to pay your dues!

Miscast EA's aren't likely to just give up on their desire to be part of artistic productions and bold new projects. But often they have to work as waiters, bartenders, clerks, or baristas, at least for a while, until something more fitting surfaces. They don't mind working simply for the paycheck as long as they have the chance to be involved in the arts scene or to pursue other creative interests in their spare time. Those kinds of activities are what they truly live for. An EA who can room with a few college friends, work a part-time job, and spend many hours a week working to promote some friends' improvisational theater troupe can feel fulfilled—at least for a time.

Unless they live in a major center for entertainment, publishing, or fashion, EA's might have to settle for a job that can accommodate only part of their desire to orchestrate and sell people on creative projects or productions. For example, a job in public relations, as long as it's working for a group or a company that allows you to take some risks and do something original, can be a decent fit, allowing an EA to do things such as plan product rollouts and press events, formulate a media strategy, and use creative techniques to get the word out about a product, service, or organization. Other business-oriented jobs, including business ownership or a consultation practice, can provide some of the same opportunities. Other EAs, meanwhile, will find that they're unwilling to make that compromise, and they'll never feel quite right unless they move to one of those big artistic meccas where they can at least make a run at becoming one of the major power players.

Picture Yourself as a Producer

A producer—whether in theater, film, or television—has the purest blend of Enterprising and Artistic traits you're likely to find. In this career, you'll apply your boundless energy and creativity to developing a winning plan for a production, then getting the right people and funding in place to make it happen. For every one idea that becomes a Broadway play, an HBO series, or an acclaimed film, thousands fizzle before they ever see the stage or the studio, and hundreds more are produced but don't go far. That means intense pressure and competition and lots of rejection and failure. However, it also means tantalizing opportunities for those shrewd enough to know a winning production when it comes along, skilled enough to sell their ideas, and disciplined enough to see things through.

You may develop and champion a new television show (or even a new type of show). You may turn an award-winning book into a riveting movie, seeking out the perfect screenwriter and cast to pull it off. You may fall in love with the script for a play and spend many months or even years selling others on its potential, hoping to get the funding you need to bring it to the stage.

When your productions succeed, you get the ultimate sense of satisfaction. The project you championed through all the trials, all the ups and downs, has finally made it before the public, and you feel vindicated. You bask in the accolades, soak up all the publicity, and love the new attention you get from people you run into at cocktail parties and industry events.

Many people who wind up as producers first have other roles in the entertainment industry; sometimes they're actors, writers, business managers, press agents, or other behind-the-scenes players. They learn the ropes and watch for their opportunity to helm their own productions.

EA Education Requirements

Most EA jobs require a bachelor's degree. However, only a few EA's go on for advanced training, because they'd rather dive in and start doing things. This works out fine, because most EA jobs and fields require specialized work experience rather than a master's degree.

EA Job Opportunities

There are fewer jobs for EA's than for any other E Code-Combo. Because of the artistic component, these jobs can come and go rapidly. Many last only for the duration of particular projects.

Because EA jobs often involve advertising, promotion, fashion, style, or design, most EA jobs are concentrated in large metro areas, especially New York and Los Angeles. Others are scattered around the country, but in many cases those are on a smaller scale and may not pay much. EA's who can tolerate, understand, and use business concepts (such as statistical studies) will have additional job options and opportunities.

EA Celebrity

Oprah Winfrey, TV host and media producer

Oprah Winfrey is an EA. She is powerful, influential, and imaginative. Winfrey is a TV personality, producer, actress, and philanthropist, best known for hosting her award-winning talk show, *The Oprah Winfrey Show*, which became the highest-rated program of its kind in history. With the encouragement of Roger Ebert, she took her show to syndication. She was able to start her own production company because of the success and the amount of revenue the show generated. By the early 1990s, she was considered to be the richest woman in entertainment. She ended her show after twenty-five years to focus on her own cable television network, OWN.

> *Passion is energy. Feel the power that comes from focusing on what excites you.*
>
> —Oprah Winfrey

ES Enterprising/Social: The Ambassador

The ES credo: *Diplomacy is the art of letting someone else have your way.*

If you're Enterprising/Social (ES), you're probably...

- *diplomatic.* You are tactful and know when to hold your tongue.
- *a mover and shaker.* You're always out there shaking hands and kissing babies.

- *overextended.* You often bite off more than you can chew.
- *a great communicator.* You know how to keep people engaged and get your ideas across.
- *popular.* Of course you're popular. You like people and have excellent social skills.
- *resourceful.* You know no stranger; therefore, you have an "in" almost anywhere.
- *a talented soft seller.* You're a smooth operator who knows how to sell ideas, concepts, and services without pushing them down people's throats.
- *a glad-hander.* You can work a room with the best of them.
- *relationship centered.* You know how to win friends and influence people.
- *community oriented.* You rarely miss a ribbon cutting.

The ES Brain

If, in the world of deal making, the EI's are the brains and the ER's are the muscle, that makes the ES's the connective tissue. This CodeCombo is characterized by a keen ability to understand people and to read them quickly. An ES is interested in using this talent to bring people together, whether for the benefit of a company, organization, government, or the community at large.

An ES wants to be out working with people, meeting and greeting, forming new bonds and connections. And these interactions are most fulfilling when they are part of achieving a broader goal. The excitement of seeing big results from people working together is a huge thrill for an ES, and that's even more so when it betters the lives of others.

If you're an ES, you are a joiner. You want to be part of service clubs, governing bodies, or groups where people share a common interest—and you have many interests. You might be part of the neighborhood association, the Rotary Club, the student council, the AIDS walk committee, the Friends of the Library board, or campus political groups. Or, if you're not already involved, these sound like the kind of things that would interest you. These types of activities are ways to get together with people who don't want to just sit on the sidelines. ES's want to be involved. And these groups appeal to you not just because you care, but also because they're great places to get to know people, find and maintain contacts or business relationships, and gain influence.

You love to win people over. This is what makes ES's good deal makers. You're always looking for an angle to gently lead people. You know that you can get people to see it your way if you can just find the right way to reach them. Yet you're not pushy or abrasive about it. That's not your style. You're more of a soft seller. This is true in conversations with friends and acquaintances, where you're willing to hear everybody out but without giving up your position. It's also true professionally, where others are sometimes stunned when they find themselves agreeing with you even when they didn't expect to.

The symbols of your achievement and your involvement are important to you. Your workspace at home or at work is likely decked out with framed certificates and diplomas, as well as photos, trophies, and other mementos of causes or committees in which you have been involved.

How ES's Relate to Others

Seemingly everyone in your community, field, or organization knows you. They see you as a leader. You are rewarded by being elected to office or selected as festival royalty. (You don't mind wearing the hokey outfit as long as you are riding in the car that leads the parade, for you know this publicity is helpful to the cause.)

Most Social CodeCombos are motivated in large part by a genuine desire to help other people, and ES's are no exception. However, more than other S combos, ES's have a healthy drive to help themselves, as well. They're good at marketing themselves. They're good at working a crowd and making sure that everybody remembers their name when they leave. ES's see the goals of helping themselves and helping others as complementary. The more personal capital the ES gains, the more he or she can help others. At work or school, ESs like to work independently more than other S CodeCombos, but they're quick to call in others to help when needed and are known as good collaborators.

If you're an ES, you're diplomatic and like to maintain a positive and upbeat work environment by treating all your coworkers with respect. Because you're a relationship builder by nature, you befriend your coworkers or classmates as well.

Your greatest strength can also be a weakness. Because you're so relationship centered, you may need a hand with your paperwork or some of the other finer points of your job. If you're a student, you may be great at working with a group to plan a project and brainstorm ideas, but you'd rather leave it to somebody else to write up the report.

The Miscast ES

As you might imagine, the kind of person we're describing needs to be on the go, making connections and working the crowds in order to feel content. Experts say that introverts are nourished by time alone, while extroverts are nourished by time with others. Well, an ES is a highly extroverted CodeCombo, and a lot of time spent in seclusion will make most ES's long for nourishment.

But it's not only ESs who get stuck behind a desk without a lot of interaction who are miscast. ESs are also likely to be frustrated by jobs that give them plenty of chances to work with people but not the authority to make deals or the latitude to develop the relationships on their own terms. ES's are exceedingly confident in their own abilities and generally chafe under tight rules and restrictions. They need to do things their way, because they know their way works.

Regardless of where ES's work, it's practically impossible to keep their Enterprising and Social tendencies completely suppressed. An ES who isn't feeling fulfilled at work will divert more energy into efforts outside of work. That might include running a side business or pitching in at a nonprofit. ES's by nature are excellent fundraisers, whether they're raising capital for a business venture or helping a social service organization wrangle money to do good works. Depending on his or her interests, an ES might also be active in politics (where the ability to size people up and persuade them is the Midas touch), a religious organization, a youth sports league, or an alumni organization. To feel a sense of purpose, ES's need the chance to use their people skills to make things happen; this makes them feel connected to their communities and fills them with pride in their accomplishments.

Picture Yourself as a Politician

Being a politician isn't the safest and easiest of careers. Whether it's the local school board, the state legislature, or even national office, there are few jobs, most don't pay a living wage, the hours are long, and the pressure is high. To top it off, the political winds are always shifting, and all it takes is one bad election campaign to end a career—or at least create an unexpected detour.

But for an ES, there's also no better way to use the gifts we've been talking about: the ability to connect with people, get them to believe in you, bring them together, and do a job that actually makes a difference on their behalf. It's also got prestige, which is irresistible to an ES.

You don't have to be an officeholder to work in politics, of course. There are campaign staff members, political strategists, lobbyists, and others. These jobs also have the elements that would be attractive to an ES.

If you're in politics, you are continually on the move, physically and mentally. Your appointment calendar is full, and it is not uncommon for you to spend your entire day going from meeting to meeting. You are always on the go and in the know. Your phone is always ringing. Actually, you probably have multiple phones so you never miss a call. You will always answer the phone—even if you're at home watching a movie with your family. You work long hours, and the line between your work and your personal life is often blurry.

You love being a community icon. Some people call you a schmoozer, but you feel a genuine responsibility to make everyone feel welcome. You enjoy being engaged and involved; in fact, the way you look at it, there is no other way to be.

When you're in politics, the next campaign is always around the corner. If it's not an election campaign, it's a campaign to get a bill or initiative passed or a campaign to raise awareness about an issue. This kind of action is invigorating to you. It's thrilling to know that there's always something new happening and that you will have the opportunity to turn your ideas into reality if you can reach enough people—which you're convinced you can.

ES Education Requirements

Most ES's are drawn to four-year colleges. Since ES's are so social and community centered, a college campus is their oyster. Some don't want to leave and end up hobnobbing with administrators, thus winning "prominent student leader" awards. Many ES jobs are in the fields of education, community leadership, and nonprofit organizations, which require at least a bachelor's degree.

ES Job Opportunities

ES's have many job opportunities. They naturally have huge networks of friends and acquaintances, which help them find and change jobs with relative ease. Some ES positions are salaried; others are commission driven. Because ES's are such schmoozers, they can often do extremely well selling products and services, especially those that help better the world.

ES Celebrity

Dr. Martin Luther King, clergyman, civil rights leader

Dr. Martin Luther King was an ES. He was inspiring, invigorating, and compassionate. King started as a Baptist preacher, becoming involved in the civil rights movement early in his career. He led the Montgomery bus boycott and became the first president of the Southern Christian Leadership Conference. He was awarded the Nobel Peace Prize. He is known as a great orator. He delivered his "I Have a Dream" speech at the 1963 March on Washington.

> *I have a dream that one day this nation will rise up and live out the true meaning of its creed: We hold these truths to be self-evident, that all men are created equal.*
> —Dr. Martin Luther King

EC Enterprising/Conventional: The Director

The EC credo: *The only way to reach your long-range goals is through achieving your short-range objectives.*

If you're Enterprising/Conventional (EC), you're probably...

- *business minded.* You're able to figure out and do whatever it takes to get things done.
- *competitive.* The whole world is your playing field—and you play to win.
- *a workaholic.* You are the first to arrive at the office and the last to leave.
- *managerial.* With the right system and structure, you feel you can get the most out of people.
- *efficient.* You can move from one transaction or subject to the next.
- *an excellent time manager.* You know when to give more and when to move on.
- *intense.* You will stop at nothing to get a perfect final product.
- *successful.* Your work ethic helps pull you to the upper rungs of the career ladder.
- *bossy.* Somebody has to take charge of others, and you're a natural.
- *a taskmaster.* You derive pleasure in compiling the to-do list.

The EC Brain

EC's are fans of order, logic, and routine. There's a right way to do things and a wrong way, and if someone does something the wrong way, he or she is likely to hear about it from an EC. Es are builders, in a sense: their drive is to create something that will bring wealth, notoriety, power, change, or all of the above. EC's are no exception. They want their efforts to result in something significant. They're not satisfied with the status quo, and they're always looking for ways to make things better. But while other Es are bold risk takers who come up with the grand plan, EC's are more likely to be the ones who mind every detail of making the plan work. And it's something they do extremely well.

If you're an EC, you have the tools to take ideas beyond the dreaming phase. When your childhood friends were talking big about building a tree house and having fun fantasizing about trapdoors, rope ladders, and secret passwords, you were with them every step of the way—but you also took the next step and figured out how much wood you'd need, where you could get it, and who among you had the skills to do each part of the job. In high school you were wanted for every prom committee and every homecoming float crew, because people knew you had the skills to get the project organized and moving toward the goal.

When people get together to work toward a goal, whether it's planning a family vacation or a corporate takeover, things can turn frustrating in a hurry. Everybody has their own ideas, people get distracted and diverted to less important tasks, and problems inevitably crop up that stall the progress. If you're an EC, you have little patience for this. You can see clearly what needs to be done, and you are willing and able to step up and take control. Before you know it, you're assigning tasks, anticipating problems, and telling your cohorts what to watch out for along the way. You're a born manager.

When there's work to be done, you are able to size up the players and the information quickly, and then tailor your approach to manage the situation, put everything together, and execute the plan. You don't shy away from complicated problems; rather, you dig in and figure out a way to make things work for everyone. You love numbers, because they provide the hard data you need to solve a problem or prove that your methods are working.

You understand that in order to make progress you must be diligent and persistent. The survivors in your field have learned that negotiation is a step-by-step process. The data is analyzed, differences are addressed, tasks are delegated, deadlines are identified, negotiation occurs, and the project is complete.

Your work is often transactional and contractual, which means you are the ultimate paper pusher and closer, all in the same body. Objectives and progress all get your adrenaline pumping. You love the art of organization, and it's invigorating to finalize the project and move on to the next one. You appreciate efficiency. You love making lists and crossing things off. While other E's are largely motivated by money, EC's can be satisfied with less tangible rewards, such as recognition, praise, and the satisfaction of a job well done.

How EC's Relate to Others

As an EC, you are a natural-born manager. You have a gift for seeing what needs to be done and delegating the necessary tasks to others. You keep a close watch over how people are doing their tasks, and as long as they're making progress, you don't get too edgy. But you can get frustrated and even fired up if work isn't getting done, and others will quickly learn that they'd better meet your standards or be called out on it.

People see you as outgoing, because you don't hesitate to charge into a situation and step up to a leadership position. It's more important to you to achieve a goal than it is to tiptoe around people's feelings. Focused on the task at hand, you zero in on what needs to be done and can feel confounded when others fail to see it the same way.

Because you naturally focus on the objective, you appreciate it when others attend to details. But you will make sure you have an understanding of the technology used in a project or the history behind the situation—you will have done your homework.

Just as you have high expectations for yourself, you probably demand the same from the people around you. You can get very frustrated if others don't do things efficiently, swiftly, and properly, and you have no patience for laziness. That means you might be seen as a control freak by some. Others—you'd consider them the ones who understand you—appreciate that you keep people on task and will gladly fall in line behind you.

The Miscast EC

While it's true that most CodeCombos won't be happy long in a job that's not the right match, the effect is exaggerated for ECs. They need jobs where they have some authority to direct other people as well as make their own decisions. Otherwise, they'll quickly work their way up to such a position or seek it with another employer.

For EC's, fulfillment comes from achieving things through careful planning and diligent follow-through. It's satisfying to map out a strategy, set the plans in motion, and, most importantly, see it succeed. If you're an EC working as an entry-level employee, you're not going to be able to take it for long. The length of time you survive is probably equal to the amount of time you exercise control over your small sphere at work—for instance, you might not be able to run the department, but you compensate by insisting on tight control over the things that are under your purview, and you get some satisfaction from orchestrating the parts of your job you can control. You might invent your own system for processing paperwork and refine it constantly to get it just right, or you might take on a de facto leadership role with coworkers even if you don't have the job title.

Picture Yourself as a Manager of an Insurance Agency

As a manager, there is always a goal to meet, always a challenge to overcome, and always a lot of people out there who might be clients if you and your team do your job right. And you love it.

It's your job to oversee a team of agents. You carve out the geographical territory. You track the team's progress. You step in to correct them, motivate them, or reward them, depending on what's needed at the moment. Those who aren't willing to get with the program won't be around long, because you have no patience for troublemakers.

You take pride in meeting the goals set for you, and you know that your superiors see you as a vital cog in the machinery of the organization. When you stride into a meeting to present a PowerPoint of your team's success, you know that people are impressed by your results, and it's that feeling that keeps you going.

Competition is fierce, especially in lean economic times, but you will do whatever it takes to get the needed contribution or the signature on the bottom line. You feel the responsibility lies on your shoulders.

You help keep office supply stores in business. Because your work is so transactional, you have many file cabinets and innumerable file folders. Your office is full of mailing lists, promotional materials, files, forms, contracts, notecards, and of course your computer. Because you are on the move, people may see you with electronic gadgets in your ears and a laptop in your briefcase.

EC Education Requirements

Some EC careers—those in retail or real estate, for example—can be built solely through work experience and/or a two-year degree, but many upper-level positions require at least a bachelor's degree. EC's who want to climb the company ladder to upper-management positions should plan on completing at least a four-year degree. Those who want to specialize in areas such as management, human resources, or nonprofit administration should earn a relevant master's degree as well.

EC Job Opportunities

A huge number of jobs are available to EC's, across all educational levels. EC's are often responsible for logistics, whether these involve people, products, or services. They manage and move business operations forward. EC's fill many middle- and upper-management positions, making upward mobility especially available to EC's. EC's are rarely consultants. Though they may work alone, they're not likely to own their own businesses. Instead, they typically work within a larger organization.

EC Celebrity

Secretary of State Hillary Clinton

Hillary Clinton is an EC. She is commanding, persistent, and disciplined. Clinton was chosen as secretary of state in the Obama administration. Prior to her appointment, she was a US senator from New York from 2001 to2009. She is the wife of Bill Clinton, the forty-second president of the United States, and the first First Lady to hold a postgraduate degree with her own professional career at the time she entered the White House. She is regarded as the most openly empowered presidential wife in America since Eleanor Roosevelt.

Voting is the most precious right of every citizen, and we have a moral obligation to ensure the integrity of our voting process.

—Hillary Clinton

Connect with other "E's" & resources online at
www.CareerCode.com/E

CHAPTER 9

Conventional (C): The Organizers

You could make a compelling case that the main thing defining civilization is organization. People organize into communities. They use a planned, organized system of agriculture to get the food they need. They organize a system of currency that people use to meet their wants and needs. They organize groups of people to perform important tasks, like providing education, producing products, administering justice, and compiling knowledge in libraries and museums.

And within these organizations are the people who are the "keepers" and the "organizers." They're the ones who keep it all from falling apart. If somebody doesn't keep track of the students, figure out how to balance the budget, and get a lesson plan in place, the education system fails. If somebody doesn't track the inventory, keep costs down, and enforce the safety rules, the factory turns into anarchy. If somebody doesn't police the streets and keep track of the rules, the justice system collapses. If nobody keeps records or arranges the books and the artifacts in an accessible form, the libraries and museums crumble. So you could say that people whose primary Interest Code is C, or Conventional, are no less than the people keeping civilization alive.

Okay, so it might be a bit of an overstatement—but not by much. It's not that other Interest Codes would be helpless to maintain order if they didn't have C's around, but it is true that C's have a special ability almost every organization in every field finds essential. They are the ones you can trust with the details. They're the budget writers, the bean counters, the inspectors, and the enforcers. They turn sloppiness into precision, waste into efficiency, and chaos into order.

If your first code is C, then you are very likely…

- organized
- detail oriented
- structured
- precise
- responsible
- careful

The C Interest Code

C's value efficiency and order above all else. They keep accurate records, develop and control a budget, and work with numbers. They can manage and take care of details, collect and organize things, and do high-quality work within a standardized framework. C's are conscientious and cautious by nature, avoiding risk. They value policies, procedures, definitions, deadlines, and systems.

C's need to know the who, what, where, when, and how of everything. Most of all, C's need to know what is expected of them and what they can expect from others. C's are the only workers who actually read the entire company manual. Most C's like clean work spaces, color-coded file folders, and well-stocked office supply rooms.

C's don't like surprises. They want to know what they are walking into each day. But C's are diligent and capable workers who willingly shoulder a great deal of responsibility. C's adore Microsoft Outlook because it manages their emails, their appointments, their address books, and their calendars.

C's are the glue (and the staples) that hold the world together. They are essential both on the front lines and behind the scenes. Because of the C's earnest and ongoing efforts and their strong operational focus, things run smoothly. Without C's, nothing would get scheduled, followed up on, or paid for.

How C's Can Get in Trouble

C's get upset when other people don't follow the rules. Often they take this rule breaking personally. Sometimes C's get snippy and judgmental with coworkers, which puts them off or chases them away. A psychologist might say that C's have major control issues.

C's have trouble just relaxing and enjoying the moment. They tend to bite off more than they can chew and, as a result, often feel pressured and overloaded. Yet C's rarely ask for help and tend to isolate themselves from others. Some C's even become martyrs, pushing too hard and feeling sorry for themselves as they think they are the only ones handling what needs to be done.

Education for C's

Many C jobs—such as medical coder, legal secretary, and traffic manager (the person who manages workflow)—require very specialized and focused training, often in programs leading to two-year associate degrees. Other C jobs may require nothing more than on-the-job training, although some do require a bachelor's degree. Some C jobs require education beyond a four-year degree, such as those in the business and museum industries.

C CodeCombos

- CR: The Inspector
- CI: The Analyst
- CA: The Curator
- CS: The Coordinator
- CE: The Regulator

CR Conventional/Realistic: The Inspector

The CR credo: *Leave no stone unturned.*

If you're Conventional/Realistic (CR), you're probably…

- *a rule follower.* The rules are there for a reason, and following them keeps things running smoothly.
- *obedient.* Nobody has to tell you twice.
- *concrete.* Meetings, bills, and taxes are real, not theoretical.

- *orderly and organized.* You feel better knowing where things are and what's expected of you.
- *steady and focused.* Some people call you a plodder, but slow and steady wins the race. Anyway, someone's got to do the day-to-day grinding.
- *predictable.* You take your coffee break at the same time each day.
- *structured.* If you're not sure of something, you check the employee handbook.
- *dependable.* You won the perfect attendance award in school. You don't let others down.
- *repetitive.* Doing the same thing at the same time each day doesn't bother you. In fact, it makes your day run smoothly.
- *stable.* You're not one for drama.
- *detail oriented.* If the recipe says three-quarter cup, that means a perfectly packed and level three-quarter cup.
- *confrontational.* If people break a rule or procedure, you'll be the first to turn them in or the first to let them know.

The CR Brain

On the night before the first day of school, did you gather all your school supplies, check them carefully against the supply list, neatly label all the folders and notebooks, sharpen all the pencils, bundle it all up in your backpack, and set it by the door so it was ready for the morning?

When you got your first desk job, were your coworkers astounded by how quickly you organized the space for maximum efficiency? And did they remain amazed by how neat your desk was kept each day thereafter, without so much as a stray Post-it Note?

These are two common hallmarks of a CR. If you're a CR, you're the kind of person who never hesitates to get out the company manual—you know the rules, and protocol and procedures aren't decoration. They're meant to be followed. You thrive on repetition, procedure, and structure. You do your best at meetings and events that have been scheduled in advance. You believe they had better be productive and worth your time. You are great at organizing files, stocking and tracking products on shelves, and catching mistakes. A lot of people put "attention to detail" among their strengths on a résumé; in your case, it's actually true.

Whether you're organizing your kitchen, compiling your tax documents, or keeping track of all your friends' birthdays, you've developed a reputation for being on top of everything. Projects with a clear beginning and end appeal to you, because you like it when things are well-defined.

All this talk of being organized may make it sound like CR's are just annoyingly anal retentive. But you know that being organized isn't just about compulsion or personal satisfaction—it's also about doing your work well and efficiently.

You like calendars, notebooks, mini-pencils with erasers, storage boxes with labels, shelves, file folders, plastic baggies, and cabinets. Everything has a place. You like to be recognized and respected as the person who makes things work. Because you are somewhat reserved, you prefer personal recognition rather than getting an award at a large function.

How CR's Relate to Others

CR's love getting things done, and they're always quick to develop a good system for doing it. That means working independently is appealing. It's not that they dislike people; it's just that it's usually simpler to do it alone rather than have to explain the system or get irritated when somebody else doesn't follow the rules.

The strong Realistic quality of CR's makes them straight shooters. They aren't usually shy about telling it like it is. A CR would see this as a positive trait, not a defect, but others may be taken aback by it. This might be confounding to a CR, who doesn't see any other desirable way. Sugarcoating things doesn't do any good; if a friend asks a CR to read her paper and it's not any good, it serves her better to get it returned covered in red marks rather than lavished with false praise. If you're a CR, you like being around the people who "get" you, and that typically means people who understand that you need to be on time, that you expect your car to be kept clean, and that doing things your way is important to you.

The Miscast CR

Luckily for C's in general, and CR's in particular, there are lots of jobs that fit them well. As we discussed, almost every organization needs people with CR traits. Even a job that isn't a pure CR job, however, can be satisfying.

A CR doesn't need to be working in a particular field to feel fulfilled; rather, he or she just needs the right role. There are usually plenty of opportunities in any job to apply the CR need for order and careful planning. If you're a CR, you may not be cut out for the social aspect of a teaching job, but you can connect with the need to keep lessons organized, your classroom tidy, and your rules firmly enforced. You may not love persuading people, but a sales job also has CR elements: the clearly defined sales goals, the need to formulate a plan of attack, the reassuring finality of a set system of prices and policies. There are matching components of many jobs for a CR.

That said, there are definitely jobs that won't feel like good fits to a CR, such as teaching and sales, just as there are with any CodeCombo. Working as a doctor might drive a CR crazy, because there can be so many possible diagnoses of the same set of symptoms—and an array of appropriate treatments. And creative jobs are too open-ended and too filled with uncertainty for a CR to feel comfortable. Being a writer or a designer who lives from gig to gig, not knowing where the next job will come from or what it will be, sounds like a nightmare to the kind of person who thrives on predictability and routines.

Picture Yourself as an Auditor

It's your job to make sure the company is running a tight ship—that the books are balanced correctly, that the right procedures are being followed, and that the annual reports are accurate. To do this, you use sophisticated software to analyze accounting records and flag any discrepancies that are found. You love to spot mistakes. You take pride in catching them, because nobody else has the persistence and determination to do it. You're respected by your coworkers because they know you're thorough and unflinchingly dedicated. If your analysis finds a problem, then it's something to be taken very seriously. You like the feeling that others recognize your talents. Your work may cause more work for them, but that's okay with you; the way you see it, you're there to save others, and they should be glad you're doing it.

When you find waste or fraud in the system, it's the ultimate "aha!" moment, like finding the needle in the haystack. You will work for hours and hours—indeed, even days, weeks , or months—for the promise of that moment when you ferret out the problems and point them out to the higher-ups. In fact, some auditors make a living as forensic auditors, working with law enforcement to investigate white-collar crimes such as embezzlement. This fits perfectly with a CR's orderly and systematic approach to work, as well as the black-and-white "follow the rules" thinking that often goes along with being a CR.

CR Educational Requirements

Most CR jobs require some technical training (typically one to two years) as well as some on-the-job training. Some CR jobs require a bachelor's degree.

CR Job Opportunities

CR's have many jobs to choose from. Many of these are entry-level and easily accessible. Most have clerical and task-oriented components.

CR's have so many options that the best way for them to narrow their job options is to select a specific industry they would like to work in.

CR Celebrity

Inspector General Patrick McFarland

Patrick McFarland is a CR. He is calculating, regulatory, and authoritative. During his twenty-two years with the US Secret Service, he coordinated protective activities for six US presidents. He also worked as a police officer and detective in St. Louis and as a special agent with the Federal Bureau of Narcotics in Chicago. McFarland has been the inspector general of the Office of Personnel Management (OPM) since August 1990. He provides leadership that is independent and nonpartisan in the pursuit of waste, fraud, abuse, and mismanagement in programs administered by OPM.

> *Poor oversight may render the national security vulnerable by allowing the employment of unsuitable persons or the granting of security clearances to individuals who would compromise the national security of the United States.*
>
> —Patrick McFarland

⬛ Conventional/Investigative: The Analyst

The CI credo: *Risk comes from not knowing what you are doing.*

If you're Conventional/Investigative (CI), you're probably...

- *attentive.* You've learned to stay present, because your work requires such focus.
- *cautious.* You don't take many risks. You have bought the same brand of peanut butter for years because you know it's tried and true.
- *contentious.* You will defend your conclusions if anyone challenges you. After all, you're sure you spent more time and effort than they did coming up with them.
- *deliberate.* You always know exactly what you're doing and why.
- *meticulous.* You wouldn't think of saying, "Close enough." You follow through, double check, and do things right.
- *judgmental.* You don't understand why everyone else can't do everything as well as you.
- *persistent.* If you can't get through to the IRS on the phone, you keep calling back every ten minutes until you get a live person on the line.
- *self-disciplined.* You're on a diet, so you refuse to eat those brownies, even if they do smell divine.

- *reserved.* Your office walls and your wardrobe are similar in color. Nothing flashy for you; that's way too distracting.
- *stable.* Anyone with your ability to juggle so many details has to have a cool head.

The CI Brain

CI's stand out from the crowd because of their ability to figure things out. They can build up a vast well of knowledge about a subject, then apply that knowledge to new situations to make an analysis or a prediction. A CI who is a baseball fan will not just watch the game. He or she will also spend hours analyzing each player's statistics as well as comparing them to their contemporaries and to past players to get a sense of whether they're overrated or underrated. This analysis will go beyond the basic statistics like batting average and RBI—a CI will find the best analytical tools available, including metrics unfamiliar to a casual fan, such as Value Over Replacement Player (VORP) or Fielding Independent Pitching (FIP). A CI knows the truth is buried somewhere in the statistics and will enjoy digging to find it.

If you're a CI, you view facts as being right or wrong. There isn't a lot of gray area. If others disagree, you might slap your forehead in frustration. Can't everybody see the plain truth right before them? You respect the rules and think everyone should follow them. There is no debate about rules. They're not suggestions.

You are organized, meticulous, and process oriented. You know how to take a project and break it down into manageable parts. You may have a gift for analyzing numbers, charts, records, figures, contracts, reports, or maps. If you play the stock market, you don't follow hunches—you invest only after careful analysis of companies' financial positions by sifting through quarterly and annual reports, competitors' performance, and the background of top executives.

Evaluation is a tedious task; you need to be slow and deliberate in order to be most effective. But you don't mind, because you couldn't imagine cutting corners. You like routines and doing things by the book. You hate working in loosely run situations where there is no structure. Because you need to work slowly and deliberately in order to be most effective, you do not appreciate interruptions, which break your intense concentration.

You love when you are able to find the answer that others missed. In our baseball example, you would like to start a blog to share your conclusions, using it to predict an underrated player's breakout season and crowing about it when your prediction turns out to be correct—but you probably don't have time since you are mired in ongoing analysis. You also feel a great sense of accomplishment when a project is done correctly and you have met your goal. Most of all, you love being an expert in your field.

How CI's Relate to Others

As we noted, CI's tend to be black-and-white thinkers. This serves them well in their work, where they can succeed by drawing clear lines between good work and bad, success and failure. This way of thinking, however, doesn't always work so well in personal relationships.

Friendships and romantic relationships require a certain amount of give and take as well as compromise. These things can be challenging for CI's, who sometimes believe there is only one right way of thinking about things and can't understand why others don't see it the same way. While some people can naturally put themselves in others' shoes, this takes work, discipline, and conscious effort for CI's. They can certainly succeed in relationships, but the way their mind works sometimes makes it a challenge.

At work, CI's are often catching the mistakes made by their coworkers, and this puts them in a natural position of authority; others quickly learn that the CI has credibility and clout. If you're a CI, you have mixed feelings about this. On one hand, you like the recognition that comes with it, and you enjoy ferreting out mistakes. On the other hand, you wish others were more careful, so you didn't have to babysit them.

You want to get along with your coworkers, but your work style requires such intensity and concentration, and takes up so much of your energy, that you have very little left for socializing during or even after work. You may therefore feel misunderstood at the office, since others do not always "get" your work needs or tasks. Others do not always see the loyalty you feel for those doing a good job.

The Miscast CI

CI's feel most at home when they're working on clearly defined projects, preferably ones that involve numbers, data sets, or codes such as computer programming languages. There are plenty of jobs that at least tangentially involve numbers, and many of them might be at least superficially satisfying for a CI, but a good fit also has elements of exploration and investigation, and preferably a good deal of authority. A job that's too repetitive and doesn't provide a chance to analyze and draw conclusions from numbers won't keep a CI engaged for long, because CI's have a need to not just interact with numbers but understand what they mean in a broad context.

So, for instance, compiling data on arrival and departure times for an airline might quickly bore a CI. But a job as an analyst who digs deep into the numbers, compares them to past performance and competitors' data, and searches for ways to improve them—now you're talking to a CI.

There are also plenty of jobs that are obvious poor fits for CI's. Artistic and social jobs are probably the worst. It's unlikely that anybody with strong CI tendencies would go down those career paths, because they simply wouldn't sound appealing. But if CI's do give them a try, their rigid way of thinking is a pretty good bet for frustration, because those kinds of jobs often have ill-defined boundaries and rules and require lots of flexibility.

Picture Yourself as a Budget Analyst

As companies and governmental bodies look for ways to get the most for their money—an ongoing process that gets more urgent during lean times—they turn to budget analysts, who help create and analyze budgets in the most efficient way possible. As a budget analyst, you receive preliminary budgets from department heads or other managers, then check them for accuracy and completeness. You ensure the budgets are written by the book and adhere to the company or governmental procedures, a crucial step in order to avoid trouble with another C CodeCombo—the auditor!

You also analyze your organization's past performance and keep tabs on what the market and your competitors are up to, always trying to stay a step ahead in finding new ways to beef up the bottom line by increasing the inflow or decreasing the outflow of cash. You exercise power when it's time for the decision makers to adopt budgets. You issue recommendations that could determine if a budget request is approved or denied. Depending on whether you're in the public or private sector, you may find yourself involved in writing legislation that involves budget matters. And your job isn't over when the budget is adopted. You're there all year long, monitoring activities and making sure budgets are executed according to the plan.

Because much of your work involves verifying the work of others, you have a tendency to be critical, although you are usually very hard on yourself as well. Despite working behind the scenes as part of a team, you do the actual tasks of your job independently without a lot of interaction from other team members. As a result, you maintain a low profile at work.

CI Education Requirements

Most CI fields of study—finance, public policy, insurance—include some type of analysis, and nearly all CI jobs require at least a bachelor's degree. Because most CI's want to find a niche or specialty within a particular field, they often earn specialized master's degrees as well.

CI Job Opportunities

CI's are critical employees in many industries; therefore, CI's typically have many opportunities once they find their specialties. Nevertheless, CI's need to be patient in building their careers. There are very few entry-level CI jobs. CI's often have to start out in other jobs and work their way into analyst positions. Once CI's obtain such positions, they usually settle comfortably into them and don't do a lot of job switching. In general, CI's do not enjoy the job search process. However, many executive recruiters are actively looking to place CI's with strong skills and experience in high-level jobs.

CI Celebrity

Abby Joseph Cohen, stock analyst

Abby Joseph Cohen is a CI. She is thorough, conscientious, and studious. Cohen is an economist and financial analyst. She works on Wall Street as a partner and senior US investment strategist at Goldman Sachs; she previously held a chief investment strategist position with Goldman Sachs. In 2001, the *Ladies' Home Journal* named her as one of the top thirty most powerful women.

> *Equity prices can rise, despite decelerating profit growth and moderately rising interest rates, if investors expect economic expansion to continue. In previous such cases, stocks outperformed bonds, often notably.*
> —Abby Joseph Cohen

CA Conventional/Artistic: The Curator

The CA credo: *Whatever is worth doing is worth doing well.*

If you're a CA, you're probably...

- *a great homemaker.* Martha Stewart is your role model. You love cooking and cleaning.
- *a perfectionist.* Everything in your living room matches perfectly and is at just the right angle.
- *precise.* You hate vague concepts. And you'd rather paint little dots than huge sweeps of color.
- *impatient.* You've been known to take away people's plates before they're done eating.
- *good at pulling things together.* You can turn chaos into order.
- *interested in structure.* No winging it for you. You want a plan and clear steps.
- *anxious.* Your need for order can make you feel threatened by disorder.
- *traditional.* You were the only one who got an A in your sewing class.
- *organized.* You know what's in every drawer in your home, and every shoe box is labeled.
- *pressed, neat, and clean.* Your prize possession is your professional steamer.
- *proper.* No free forming for you. You'd prefer to work from a pattern.

The CA Brain

The CA is another of those CodeCombos that combines two codes that usually don't mix well. The C is all about rules, procedures, and systems. The A is all about creativity, expression, and experimentation. These two seemingly competing tendencies find a middle ground in people who love beauty and creativity but find it satisfying to impose order upon it in one way or another. Think needlepoint, beading, and cross-stitch.

A classic result is somebody who's interested in collecting art objects: paintings, coins, clothing, postcards, old books, carvings. A CA is interested in learning everything there is to know about one set of objects—often a narrow subset, such as Renaissance poetry or the art of China's Ming dynasty. Appreciating the collection is a pleasure, but so is categorizing it, organizing it, and caring for it.

If you're a CA, you like things to be orderly and systematic. Doing things right is your goal—this is what gives you the greatest sense of accomplishment. You're a master of your space. You like to hang onto things that others might throw away, but you always know where all your things are, even if others have a hard time understanding your system. And you're protective; as a kid, you wanted to put up signs everywhere saying, "Don't touch my stuff!" Prying siblings or friends would just mess things up.

Even though you're organized, you're not the type to have everything neatly stacked and filed, like other C's might be. You understand the statement "My office is clean underneath." You might have a cluttered space because you feel you have to hang onto everything—but your office was spotless before you started that pile of newspapers and that stack of maps and that bin full of magazines. In fact, if you're like many CA's, you may operate in a system of piles.

In general, you feel comfortable with rules. There are certain tried-and-true methods to use for preserving, organizing, and accessing the things that are important to you, and these need to be followed by everyone.

The perfectionist part of you likes to weed out things that should be discarded, repaired, or replaced—but you have difficulty getting rid of these things until absolutely necessary, because you might need something for a future project. In some instances you are conflicted. When you *are* able to get rid of something, anything you give away will be in great shape, clean, and repaired. You've been known to get a late start on projects because you get caught up in preparations. You'll spend time collecting the right pieces and tools to do the project. Then you'll read the manual or the detailed instructions. Finally, you will begin. You work slowly because everything has to be done right.

How CA's Relate to Others

Sometimes working with others is a challenge for you. For one thing, you probably do many things yourself in order to make sure they are done right. This may leave very little for others to do. It can be difficult for you to work with a team, as the errors everyone else makes really bother you. Your coworkers may call you a control freak, but you would rather do certain things yourself and save the time it would take to correct someone else's mess.

It may be difficult for you to be an effective supervisor, as you tend to be critical of others' work—and of your own as well. You sometimes complain that you cannot get help from others, but when others do pitch in, you might complain about the quality of their work. This is the price you pay for wanting things to be done right.

The Miscast CA

If you're a CA, you have a couple of choices: you can dedicate yourself to preparing for and getting one of the few CA jobs that are available, or you can make some compromises. As we've seen, there are plenty of C jobs, so it's perfectly reasonable for somebody with the CA CodeCombo to get a job that's at least a decent match for their C Interest Code. Every organization needs people who are good at implementing and enforcing a system. Even if it's not an organization that allows you to be involved in anything artistic, it can be the kind of job a CA is reasonably happy in.

Those CA's, however, are almost certainly going to pursue something that nurtures their artistic and conventional tendencies outside of work. That could very well be a collection. You might assemble and maintain an impressive array of antique furniture pieces or your own in-home library. If you're a music fan, you're probably the type who saves CDs and their cases and stores them somewhere on display—no books full of CD sleeves or MP3 libraries for you. Or, better yet, you might like to collect mint-condition vinyl. Happily for CA's, there are plenty of opportunities to do such things, and it's not uncommon to see a CA who is far more engaged in and proud of a deeply involved hobby than anything he or she does at work.

Picture Yourself as a Historical Librarian

The books, newspapers, letters, and other documents under your care have survived decades, or even centuries, and each has its own character, historical, and artistic value. And there is no way you're going to let anything mess that up.

You can spend hours organizing and preserving items in your library or archive. You honor these materials and expect others to do the same. You enjoy analyzing and selecting items and making recommendations for new purchases or acquisitions.

You may be an expert in a very narrow field, such as Civil War documents or Russian literature. You know all the small details of the artifacts or products in question and can spend hours tracking down new potential acquisitions. You have boundless energy when you are on the hunt.

You work in a setting where there is a collection of materials others need to access, and you pride yourself in being able to protect and keep order to the collection. You feel powerful when you are able to control access to and use of the materials. You know you have to wear gloves when you touch antique treasures, and you expect others to do the same.

You love organizing and displaying the items in the collection, and you like it when others play by the rules. You enjoy telling others about the collection because this enables you to demonstrate your expertise. This is your chance at being the star in your own private show.

CA Education Requirements

Most CA jobs require four-year degrees; some, such as museum curator, require specialized master's degrees.

CA Job Opportunities

Relatively few CA jobs are available. Furthermore, most professional CA jobs are highly specialized. Typically these are found in libraries, museums, and other arts or historical depositories. CA's are also good pattern designers, art preservationists, wardrobe coordinators for theaters, and closet or garage organizers.

Many CA's do well as salespeople in some retail settings, especially those that require strong organizational abilities plus an artistic flare. Thus CA's might work in wedding invitation stores, accessory shops (where they can stack and fold beautiful scarves, hats, and gloves), needlework shops (where there are thousands of types of yarns to stack and locate), gift stores, card stores, and bead stores.

CA's like to assist with organizing art festivals, musical fundraisers, and other similar events. They design the forms, make the rules about when the forms have to be in, decide who is going to be where, and do it all for the sake of art.

CA Celebrity

Virginia Mecklenburg, senior curator for the Smithsonian American Art Museum

Virginia Mecklenburg is a CA. She is a classifier who is observant and creative. An accomplished author and lecturer, she has specialized in twentieth-century American art and organized many art exhibitions as well as authored books and magazine articles about American artists such as Edward Hopper and George Bellows. She coauthored *Metropolitan Lives: The Ashcan Artists and Their New York*.

> *With humor and pathos, they have transformed everyday experiences into stories revealing the aspirations and values that have sustained Americans through good times and bad.*
>
> —Virginia Mecklenburg,
> on the Rockwell exhibition
> created by George Lucas
> and Steven Spielberg.

CS Conventional/Social: The Coordinator

The CS credo: *Never mistake motion for action.*
—*Ernest Hemingway*

If you're Conventional/Social (CS), you're probably...

- *a systemizer.* You categorize nearly everything you encounter, which helps keep you and your company organized and put together.
- *detail oriented.* Nothing escapes your scrutiny.
- *a front liner.* You love inviting people in and showing them around.

- *efficient.* You don't believe in wasting energy or time.
- *moral.* You can be trusted with the company cashbox.
- *obedient.* You do what you're told by management—and usually with no questions asked.
- *organized.* Your desk looks like it belongs in an office furniture catalog.
- *precise.* You have all your documents organized and ready for preparing your income tax return.
- *scheduled.* Your daily planner is neatly filled in, and you follow it dutifully.
- *structured.* You live according to a plan and a routine.
- *helpful.* When someone asks for your assistance, you lend a hand.
- *something of a martyr.* You can feel responsible for the whole world if you're not careful.

The CS Brain

A CS is a unique mix: organized and kind, productive and pleasant. Most C's work in the realm of "things," whether those things are spreadsheets, dollars, or products. CS's have the same reliance on structure, but they apply it to the world of people. They are good at putting people at ease, while at the same time making sure they're in the right place at the right time. They're perfect field trip chaperones and hotel concierges.

If you're a CS, you are often put in charge of making sure things get done for people—either because it's your job or because you're so good at it that family and friends just look to you. You take your responsibilities very seriously. You are very loyal and dependable and often take the initiative to get things done.

You are comfortable with authority and like to receive appreciation from the people around you. You beam with pride when your boss, your spouse, or your friends tell you tell how important you are. You feel good knowing that they can depend on you. You like being valued and treated with respect by the coworkers or clients at work. However, if they don't follow the proper rules and procedures, you may be tempted to discount their opinion.

Regardless of your line of work, you enjoy building relationships with the customers or clients, and you like to feel like you're one of the reasons why those customers come back.

How CS's Relate to Others

You appreciate it when workplace rules and protocol are followed, and you get very frustrated when coworkers do not comply; however, it is very difficult for you to work up the courage to confront others about your "beefs." In fact, it will eat you up for days on end. You generally see the best in others and enjoy being around them. People describe you as friendly and outgoing, but you also tend to be a no-nonsense personality. You're not prone to long chats or unnecessary tangents when there are things to be done.

Typically, you work as part of a team. You are able to provide quality control for your workplace, yet you also play well with others. You present yourself pleasantly and politely, and your coworkers value this. You try to help your coworkers who play by the rules because you like to be of service; however, if they don't accept your help, or if they ignore the rules, you can become very frustrated and critical.

You place high standards on your work accomplishments and expect the same of others. If someone has made a mistake and needs help, you prefer to respond after they recognize the value of your contribution.

Cheryl's Story

From the time she was a little girl, Cheryl wanted to be a nurse. She thought caring for others was one of the most rewarding jobs around. Eventually she earned her RN and took a job at a large hospital in a midsized town. She was an incredible nurse. Her colleagues enjoyed working with her, and her supervisors thought she was the ideal employee and gave her additional responsibilities, including training new nurses.

When a nursing administrator position opened up, she was asked to apply. She was flattered, so she applied and was offered the position. After a month in her new position, she had lost nearly ten pounds. She was stressed and grouchy; she often lashed out at her colleagues who had once been her good friends. She was no longer caring for people, and she was constantly in management meetings, making decisions about patient counts or equipment inventories and having difficult conversations with the nurses who weren't performing to hospital standards. Not only did she despise the job, but her nursing colleagues began to resent her as well.

Cheryl came to Jan's office after she had been let go by the hospital. Jan tested her and found that her CodeCombo was a

CS, which made her a great fit for her bedside nursing job. She loved caring for others and being responsible for important details, and her S was sensitive to her patients who were healing. When she went to management, she had no E (Enterprising), which was necessary in order to direct and manage her fellow nurses and make tough decisions. Jan explained that many people who are good at the job they originally trained for are later tapped for management but find it a horrible fit. Cheryl felt much better after her assessment, which helped her understand why she wasn't successful in a management position, and she began to apply for nursing positions.

The Miscast CS

If you're a CS, you need that all-important contact with other people to feel fulfilled. When you have positive, helpful interactions with others, you feel a sense of purpose— you're making the world a friendlier place, where people are courteous and mindful of the needs of others. Unfortunately, there are a lot of jobs where that need doesn't get met, and a CS working in a job with limited contact with people, or in a workplace where basic courtesy isn't valued, will be logging on to job search websites before long.

The dominant C Interest Code, again, can be a saving grace for CS's, who can find themselves good jobs as valuable parts of a company by using their knack for ensuring that everything is done by the book. Still, CR or CE a miscast CS will seek a more perfect match outside of work, if it is not possible to find a matching job. CS's make great volunteers, because they like to serve and want to do things the right way—both traits that any nonprofit, church, or government group would love in a volunteer.

Picture Yourself in a College Admissions Office

In this environment, you serve an important double purpose: You're the first contact many future students will have with the college, so you must make a good first impression. You're also helping to run a crucial arm of the institution by processing applications, answering questions, and helping arrange and carry out on- and off-campus recruiting events. It's a busy life, and there's a lot to keep track of, but you're up to the task.

You work as part of a team, which provides you with clear guidance for doing your job. Rules and structure also provide you with helpful direction. You have no problem with repetitive job tasks, such as going through email or sorting documents. You take a no-nonsense approach to your job. You often deal with important minutiae, so you need to take your time to make sure you do it right the first time. You keep materials neat and orderly so they are easily accessible. You have a carefully designed system for this, perhaps involving color-coded tabs and folders.

CS Education Requirements

Because CS's are efficient, most of them want to complete their education as quickly as possible. Many CS jobs require some technical training—typically, a one- to two-year program at a technical or community college. Other CS jobs, such as business support services, require nothing more than on-the-job training. There are some high level CS jobs such as administrative assistant that require a bachelor's degree.

CS Job Opportunities

The CS role is invaluable to many organizations, especially those that need a strong administrative staff to provide excellent services to students, patients, or clients. CS jobs are plentiful. Organizations most in need of CS's include schools, clinics, and law offices, although every small business with an office probably needs a CS.

CSs tend to enter the labor market at a relatively young age. Most choose an area of specialization—such as healthcare, education, social services, or legal services—early in their career.

CS Celebrity

Emily Post, writer, authority on etiquette and manners

Emily Post was a CS. She was proper, opinionated, and considerate. Post attended Miss Graham's finishing school in New York City. After her divorce in 1905, Post focused her efforts on writing. In 1922, her book *Etiquette* became a best seller, with updated versions continuing to be popular for decades. In 1946, she founded the Emily Post Institute, which continues her work. A number of her descendants continue to write about etiquette.

Nothing is less important that which fork you use. Etiquette is the science of living. It embraces everything. It is ethics. It is honor.

—Emily Post

CE Conventional/Enterprising: The Regulator

The CE credo: *In God we trust—all others we audit.*

If you're Conventional/Enterprising (CE), you're probably…

- *highly accurate.* You take great pride in your precision and correctness.
- *disciplined.* You keep a tight schedule so you can get everything done.
- *industrious.* Because of your diligence and hard work, you never miss a deadline.
- *focused.* Nothing gets by you.
- *a governor.* You put a stop to negative trends before they get out of hand.
- *internally focused.* You spend a lot of time in your own thoughts.
- *anal.* At least that's what others say about you, just because you're extremely particular.
- *a recognition seeker.* You work hard for others and make sure you tell them so.
- *pushy.* You prefer the term "assertive."
- *reliable.* You never have to be asked twice.
- *responsible and trustworthy.* There's no slack, doubt, or wiggle room in what you do.

- *honest.* Make that incorruptible.
- *tightly wound.* The pressure on you can feel nearly overwhelming at times.

The CE Brain

Knowledge is power, and CE's like having this advantage because in their ideal job they are directing or coordinating some type of program. Job-specific knowledge is their operational base. Like other CEs, you enjoy structure, stability, and predictability, in a job and at home. You take comfort in being surrounded by detailed rules, procedures, policies, and regulations. You appreciate the prestige of bona fide accomplishment. A CE is confident and assertive, more so than other C CodeCombos. While other C's may be understood as applying organization and structure to their sphere of the world, a CE is the one most likely to go out and police others who may need—ahem—a little help following the rules.

You value the concept of a fair playing field, and seeing people work the system for their own advantage drives you crazy. Nobody should get special breaks. You deeply appreciate receiving an award—*if* it is given selectively and for excellent work. You would rather receive no award than one that doesn't mean much. You always take a conservative approach, whether you're looking for an apartment, planning a budget, or even dating. Taking things slowly and carefully, and having all the facts in hand, helps avoid painful mistakes. You do not like to take risks.

Time management is not an issue for you. Most of the projects you lead will have a clear beginning and an end; if not, you make it so in order to meet deadlines. In the face of these demands, you may need to become focused and very directive with workers or consultants involved in your project until it is finished.

How CE's Relate to Others

People know you as reliable and clearheaded, and they appreciate that you can be counted on. You're not so sure about them. You see yourself as highly competent, and you sometimes look down on those who don't rise to the same standard or work as hard as you do.

You know that you can come off as pushy or unconcerned about others, but you don't mean any offense. It's not that you don't care about other people; you're just caught up in whatever you're working on, and you don't feel the need to humor people who can't keep up with you.

Interruptions during high-stress times are quite annoying, and you may become short-tempered with others who try to interact with you. You can be difficult to work with because you can become so focused and feel a lot of internal pressure. You can be judgmental of your coworkers. If you are in a position of power, you may have a reputation for mowing people down when they don't do things correctly.

The Miscast CE

A CE with talents who does not have the right outlet can become a train wreck. A combination of rigidity and a lack of inhibition about informing others of their mistakes can lead to workplace conflicts, as you might well imagine.

CE's enjoy being insiders who are part of the action behind the scenes. They like knowing that not everybody gets to do what they do. So a run-of-the-mill kind of job as a retail manager or an administrative assistant is not a cup of tea for most CE's.

Jobs that don't provide enough of a management challenge are another red flag. If you're a CE, you see yourself as able—and with good skills—and you feel it's your mission to use your abilities, because they will be of obvious benefit to society or business. You like the challenge of entering a fresh situation, figuring it out, and finding flaws to fix in order to keep things running smoothly.

Picture Yourself as a Government Regulator

It's your job to check and double-check to make sure all the rules are being followed. You might do this for banks, for nursing homes, for insurance companies, or for trucking companies. All have sets of regulations they need to follow, and that means somebody needs to make sure they're enforced. Your job requires you to keep up-to-date on laws and best practices, and you commit them to memory and can cite chapter and verse when necessary.

The day-to-day flow of your work might involve site visits to do interviews or visual inspections, or it might involve poring over documents, depending on what industry you're regulating. You may be on the go, but you also have a quiet desk where you can concentrate and do the paperwork that maintains order and compliance.

You know that your job is important and that a lot of people have an interest in what you're doing. Some people would try to influence you or play you if they can, but you're straightforward and honest, partly because your principles demand it and partly because you like being in a position of power and aren't about to compromise that.

CE Education Requirements

Most CE jobs require a bachelor's degree or advanced specialization, which can include graduate school. In order to maximize advancement opportunities and earning potential, most CE's need to complete their education before or early in their career.

CE Job Opportunities

The employment opportunities for CE's are vast. CE skills are needed in every field to handle regulation, record keeping, compliance, contracts, and administrative tasks.

CE Celebrity

William K. Black, bank regulator

William Black is a CE. He is dogmatic, resolute, and directive. Black is a lawyer, an academic, an author, and a former bank regulator. He is known for his expertise in white-collar crime, public finance, and regulation. He developed the concept of "control fraud," in which executives use the entities they control as "weapons" to commit fraud. He authored the book *The Best Way to Rob a Bank Is to Own One.*

We always took the position, as S&L regulators, that if we were taking enforcement action, that assuredly was something material, otherwise, we wouldn't be doing it.
　　　　　　　　　　　　　　　　　—William Black

Connect with other "C's" & resources online at
www.CareerCode.com/C

CHAPTER 10

Codes Make a Difference

Even if you and your family members share the same DNA, more than likely you will have different codes. Because of these differences, you may not face the same struggles in life or in the labor market as your parents, your family members, and your friends. It is extremely important to make a distinction between codes and people. The US Constitution states that "all men are created equal," and we concur. All people do have equal worth; unfortunately, however, the influences of their codes will create disadvantages for some and an unequal playing field for all. It is simply a fact that some codes will lead to higher paychecks, greater job availability, more career advancement opportunities, and better status among your peers. Being aware of these differences can provide the understanding and acceptance you will need to make career choices; however, it may be difficult to accept if you realize that your codes may not garner the results you or your family expects.

After studying the codes for more than eight years, we have noticed some patterns related to money, education, job availability, job search, geographical area, and promotional opportunities. We discuss these patterns below.

Money

We mention money first, because this is a major driving force propelling workers into the labor market. Most people work because they need money for themselves or their family. It is a fact that some codes will earn more than others. We have found that if you have an A or an S in your CodeCombo, your job matches will typically pay less than job matches for individuals with an E or an I in their codes. In fact, the code that leads people to have the highest earning potential is E because the jobs with the best match for Es tend to be in sales, business, and/or management. A's typically earn the least, unless they are fortunate enough to be a highly paid actor, artist, singer, designer, etc.

Education

If you have an I in your CodeCombo, nearly all your job matches will require the pursuit of postsecondary education at the baccalaureate or graduate school level. People with an I code will need to select an area of specialization and pursue many years of study to obtain the necessary vocational qualifications for a spot in the labor market. The other codes have many educational pathways to jobs, ranging from less than a high school education to graduate school.

Job Availability

There are a limited number of job opportunities if there is an I or an A in your CodeCombo, as many of these jobs require specialization or a particular talent. However, there are many jobs available to the R, C, S, and E codes.

Job Search

Your codes dictate your job search style. If you are an E, you will have an easier time during a job search than the other codes because you will be networking, selling yourself to employers, and aggressively pursuing opportunities.

If you are an R, you may have a ready-made system for job searching if you work in the trades and are a member of a labor union. If you are missing this network, you may struggle in finding job opportunities and selling yourself to an employer.

C's are natural record keepers; they manage and service their job-search activities. They not only like the structure of a job search but need it. They know when they sent their résumé, when the closing date for the job opening was, and when they should be getting a call for an interview. What they dislike is unkept promises about callbacks and timelines.

If you have an I in your CodeCombo and you are highly specialized, you may not have to search for a job at all. You will likely be listed in an employment recruiter's database of potential job applicants. The recruiters will contact you when matching openings occur. If you lack an area of specialization, you may struggle to network with the necessary people and places to find the few jobs available to you.

The A's may struggle with the formalities and the structure of a job search, but they bring uniqueness to the process; their résumé paper may be a bright color, or they may wear an unconventional outfit to the interview. A's are usually thinking about how they are going to make themselves stand out among the other candidates. Some A's have agents who lead them to project employment.

If you have an S in your code, you will likely find job opportunities through all your connections. Because S's are always checking in with one another (family and friends) or are serving their community, they are always "in the know." Not only do the S's help each other find work, they help all the other codes as well!

Geographical Area

There are some communities that have an abundance of job opportunities for particular Interest Codes. For example, Los Angeles and New York City are great areas for A's who work in entertainment or fashion design, or Es who work on Wall Street.

I's who are interested in academic ventures will need to locate in urban areas with major medical clinics and universities in order to be near research facilities and educational opportunities. Most communities, large and small, offer at least some job opportunities for R's, S's, E's, and C's. If you have an I or an A in your CodeCombo, you will find job availability increases in major cities and decreases significantly in rural markets.

Promotions

Even if you enjoy your job and are acknowledged as being one of the best employees in your organization, you may not be well suited for a promotional opportunity that includes supervision and management tasks. It is enticing to think you can earn more money as a supervisor or manager, but if you are not well suited for the pressure and the difficult decisions that might have to be made (hiring, firing, performance evaluations, confrontation), it will be best for you to remain in a job without the stress. Workers who are suited for supervision and management will typically have an E in their CodeCombo.

On the other hand, if you have a boss who is not a good match for supervisory and management tasks, you may become very dissatisfied with your job and organization. You may find other workers experiencing similar dissatisfaction, which will affect the work performance of an entire division or department.

The Six-Letter CareerCode

We have spent a lot of time discussing two-letter CodeCombos as well as describing the similarities and differences for these thirty code types. There are remarkable differences among the CodeCombos that allow us to understand the importance of our mantra, "Know your code; find your fit."

Of course, everyone really has a six-letter CareerCode—a personalization of all six codes. It would be complicated, confusing, and not really helpful to describe all the configurations for the six-letter CareerCodes. The ordering of the codes defines the CareerCodes.

Since there is a rank ordering of the six codes that produces your CareerCode, it can also be helpful to understand the influence of your last two codes in the six-letter chain. For example, if your CareerCode is ICERSA, you might want to avoid jobs where you are expected to perform human services (S) in a creative environment (A). Instead, you will prefer to work in a business environment where you are doing tasks like investigating and examining.

If your CareerCode is SRIAEC, you might want to avoid jobs where you are expected to perform management (E) and inspection (C) tasks. You will want to work with patients, clients, or customers, providing a service instead of working for the government, performing inspections and managing other workers.

If your Career Code is EASCIR, you might want to avoid jobs where you are expected to perform investigative (I) and manual (R) tasks. You will want to be on stage, performing, instead of behind the scenes, doing research and setup functions.

If you are unhappy with your job, you will be able to identify the reasons for your dissatisfaction if you know your CareerCode. This understanding allows you to make the changes necessary to improve workplace satisfaction.

CHAPTER 11

A Final Note

We hope you have gained a greater understanding of CareerCode. Did you experience an "aha" moment when you read your results?

Our intent is to validate who you are and how you contribute to the world of work. Validation is so important because it recognizes you for who you are, and gives you full permission to own it! People who feel validated usually feel empowered to go out and find the environment that best fits their unique strengths and talents.

Depending upon where you are in your career development, your results may mean different things to you. In the case of Tracy's college students, many are just beginning to develop self-awareness. Their results don't always give them an "aha" moment because they don't know themselves well enough to recognize a good fit. However, we feel it's important to plant the seeds of awareness to enable them to begin thinking about their options. Career changers may have similar experiences; often they are not quite ready to accept their codes because this may be the first time they have thought about themselves in another light. However, this information should give them permission to change the way they think of themselves in regard to the world of work.

You may have read your results and quickly understood why you have been struggling. Jan's middle-aged clients are perfect examples of those who need to understand why they have struggled, when it appears that their friends, siblings, and significant others have not. If you can identify with that scenario, think back to times in your life when you did not feel well matched in jobs, roles, or situations. Was that environment the opposite of your code? Did you work in an area that valued production and efficiency when your code valued relationships? Perhaps you were working in an environment that was more Enterprising and Conventional, when your Interest Code is Social.

In summary, we have seen several clients who are severely lacking in self-esteem and confidence, and we soon discovered how quickly that takes a toll on career decisions. Students and clients who are very shy and lack self-esteem are stuck because they often don't have a solid sense of who they are and what they can contribute. We do a lot of encouraging with these types of clients. They should not be afraid to learn about who they are.

Our greatest hope is that you received some validation from your results that have served to empower you to recognize and *own* what makes you unique. From here you can begin to measure if you are in the best environment or job for your code. Understanding who you are in relation to others helps define your fit even more. Look around and begin to identify someone you know with each of the different Interest Codes. How do they differ from you? Do they contribute skills that you don't have? Do you value what they bring to the table? More importantly, do you value your own uniqueness?

We look forward to hearing from you as you learn more and more about this theory and how to apply it to your life and your relationships. Please share your stories with us at www.careercode.com, and always remember: Know your code; find your fit!

Acknowledgments

Discovering who one is and where one fits is a part of every person's journey. We would like to thank our parents, friends, family, teachers, and mentors for helping us develop a strong sense of self-awareness and self-esteem. Because of their guidance, we've been able to help others define who they are and where they fit in the world of work and life.

Special thanks go to Tracy's mom, Carol Lungrin, whose continued interest and support, not to mention free editing, has been unforgettable and steadfast. She has been there with us every step of the way, and we cannot thank her enough. For Ron Hendren, who has read every single draft for five years, telling us each new one was better than the first: your optimism has kept us going.

Special appreciation to Dylan Belden, who helped us find our voice; Joan Holman, for all her creative insight and energy; and to Jorgy Jorgenson who blew wind into our sails when we needed it most. We also want to extend our sincere gratitude to Joan and Steve Carter as well as Stephen Clemente, who have so willingly offered their time and expertise to our project. To the remainder of our close family members and friends who have continued to be excited and supportive of us over this very extended and demanding process, we cannot thank you enough for your encouragement.

About the Authors

Jan Lowe was raised in a small Nebraska community, where she played the piano for the high school choir. She pursued a bachelor's degree in music education and was in the first year of her teaching career when she realized it was not a good match. Fortunately, after obtaining additional education and a master's degree, she found an alternative career as a vocational rehabilitation counselor, which was more fulfilling than teaching as she was able to work with individual clients rather than a classroom of students. Building on her vocational rehabilitation counseling experiences, she became specialized in vocational assessment and courtroom testimony as a vocational expert, which is very satisfying work and a good match for her CareerCode—AECISR.

Tracy Lungrin was raised in two Nebraska communities— Ogallala and Kearney. After high school, she attended the University of Nebraska at Kearney, where she earned a bachelor's degree in organizational communication and a master's degree in counseling—with a student affairs emphasis. Tracy has been working in jobs in higher education that are a great match to her SEAICR CareerCode; these have allowed her to make a living using her love for developing and maintaining relationships. She began her career as an admissions counselor and more recently worked as a fraternity and sorority advisor. She now works as a development officer for the University of Nebraska Foundation.

The authors invite you to visit www.careercode.com and share your stories and thoughts about CareerCodes and our motto, "Know your code; find your fit!"